THE SUNFLOWER SINNER
An Odyssey of Politics and Passion

Cynthia Dennis

Woodley Memorial Press
Washburn University
Topeka, Kansas

The Bob Woodley Memorial Press
Washburn University
Topeka, KS 66621
www.washburn.edu/reference/woodley-press

Cover photo: Cynthia Dennis
Book design: Paul Hotvedt, Blue Heron Typesetters
Cover design: Jeanette Pham

DEDICATION

For my family.

And for all of the other families who have ridden their own waves of chaos, George Bernard Shaw penned this tidbit:

"IF YOU CANNOT GET RID OF THE FAMILY SKELETON,
YOU MAY AS WELL MAKE IT DANCE."

ACKNOWLEDGEMENTS

It is hardly practical to offer a lengthy Academy Awards caliber list to thank all of the individuals involved in birthing my book. Among them are: manuscript critics; writing instructors; literary agents; a pair of Kansas judges; researchers at The National Archives, the Kansas State Historical Society, and the Hutchinson Library; valued friends; Paul Hotvedt of Blue Heron Typesetters; and Woodley Press's managing editor Paul Fecteau.

In compiling a memoir, its author must make certain determinations about the recall of long-ago events and conversations. For we often tend to remember them as overall impressions rather than in finite detail. With that in mind, I recreated family conversations by using typical speech patterns and oft-repeated phrases, and verified them with family members.

Accounts of the court trials were based on trial transcripts and related documents, newspaper stories, and relevant research. Documentation of political speeches and campaigns, and other historical events, was drawn from such archival records.

Pseudonyms and composite characters were used sparingly with the sole purpose of not compromising individual privacy.

It was tempting to delete certain facts that might create discomfort for my family. But I did not, believing that the truth must prevail. If we choose to deny our personal histories, we opt to hide the essence of who we are. So the truth, as I have experienced it, is represented here to the best of my ability.

THE SUNFLOWER SINNER
An Odyssey of Politics and Passion

Cynthia Dennis

TABLE OF CONTENTS

PROLOGUE	DAD WANTS TO BE GOVERNOR	1
CHAPTER 1	PECK'S BAD BOY	7
CHAPTER 2	MURDER IN THE BASEMENT	34
CHAPTER 3	THE INVINCIBLE MRS. BROWN	42
CHAPTER 4	OUR LET'S-PRETEND FAMILY	71
CHAPTER 5	A SEDUCTRESS IN PINK	97
CHAPTER 6	THE FATEFUL INQUIRY	109
CHAPTER 7	AN APRIL FOOLS' DAY BRIBE	123
CHAPTER 8	DESCENT INTO HELL	137
CHAPTER 9	THE MISTRESS AND THE IRS	161
CHAPTER 10	WHO GOT THE PAYOFF?	173
POSTSCRIPT	FAREWELL TO DASHED DREAMS	204

"In the past, those who foolishly sought power by riding on the back of the tiger ended up inside."
John Fitzgerald Kennedy

PROLOGUE

DAD WANTS TO BE GOVERNOR
1949

"MYYYY FELLOOOO REEE-PUB-LICK-UNS ... " The cadence of my father's voice lured me to huddle next to our vanilla-and-brown striped radio. Its metal dial was pointed to a station in Hutchinson. Or Hutch, as we knew the town 30 miles away down a dull stretch of Kansas pavement. Static noises crackled across the airwaves between there and our kitchen in Mac, formally known as McPherson to the uninformed. It caused me to lean closer, transforming my right ear to an appendage of the radio's mesh front.

I watched a stream of sunshine full of dancing dust motes. It slanted through a narrow kitchen window toward the radio, connecting it with the world outside. I wondered if my father was somehow attached to the shards of sun, sending his words directly to us so we could be part of his triumph.

"I THAAA-NK YOUUU FOR THIS GRAAA-TE HONOR," he droned.

Tumultuous cheers, interspersed with stomping, reverberated through the radio. "You are listening, LIVE, to the newly elected chairman of the Young Republicans of Kansas. Paul A. Lackie," the gravelly voice of an announcer informed. "WHAAAT a contest we've seen!" He went on as if to quote The Hutchinson News-Herald of the prior day. Its headline had warned:

> "Two battles are on tap ... Second comes the fight for the state chairmanship, which has developed into a 3-way pitched battle that should keep the rooms of the Bisconte hotel, convention headquarters,

1

a Technicolored blue smoke haze throughout Friday night."

My father was probably swaying by now in front of the cheering crowd, as a tall thin tree would in sufficient wind. His eyes, blue like enormous marbles flecked with black glitter, were traveling skyward. His thick lips were curled in a half smile. Threads of his fine silk suit were gleaming under the podium lights. He resembled a racehorse, shivering with the glory of appearing before the audience for which he had been groomed.

"AS YOUR NEW CHAIRRRR-MAN ... " Yelling started again. It drowned out the voice that had greeted us before breakfast each morning for weeks. We had listened to it rehearse behind a bathroom door and fine-tune the speech he long dreamed of making. I pictured him leaning on the refrigerator right there in the kitchen as my sisters and I choked down breakfast oatmeal. He spun words off his tongue between puffs on a Pall Mall. His voice stretched to eternity and wrapped us in its optimism. It promised that we were destined to stand in the winner's circle beside him and applaud along with the crowd.

"LACK-EEE, LACK-EEE," they chanted. "SHHH," Grandma Ida said to my sister Margo, who was fidgeting her sassy four-year-old body on top of a short stool. "SHHH. Your father is giving his acceptance speech."

"Don' care." She flipped defiant blue eyes, making her golden hair wave like stalks of Kansas wheat.

Andrea squatted on the floor, playing and babbling baby gibberish.

"SHHH, both of you! Listen to Dad!" I ordered, making each of my sisters glare back.

"Daaah," two-year-old Andrea yelled.

Grandma Ida picked up her squirming body, and held it tight.

* * * * *

2

My father had prepped us for this state-wide GOP chairmanship victory by preceding it with a more modest one two years before. That was when he had snared the chairmanship of the Fourth District Young Republicans of Kansas. He had captured it so effortlessly that I assumed anyone who wanted a political post could simply ask for it. He had not subjected us to incessant rehearsals of speeches, or even outlined any particular strategy for that coup. It had made me wonder whether all of his post-war lamentations about heated political contests were only window dressing.

From the start, he had promised us grand possibilities to be realized along his path to political power. As his resident patrons, we were slated to soar along behind this Pied Piper who was already flitting in and out of our lives. He was willing to share his political glories with us IF we did our part.

Once he became governor, "GUVVV-UH-NUH OF THIS GRAAA-TE STATE OF KANNN-SUS," we would travel in black limousines and shake hands with other famous men like him. In exchange, we must present exemplary public facades as those perfect daughters our mother was grooming. Our role was to be well dressed and exceedingly polite, to sit alongside our candidate wearing Ipana smiles in family political photographs, and to utter "please" and "thank you" without fail.

The daily political word pictures he painted with a flamboyant brush inevitably made my mind fly to distant places, as far as my current nine-year life span would take it. Eventually the journey led me into fantasy worlds populated with exotic celebrities, like the movie stars whose photos I clipped from <u>Modern</u> <u>Screen</u> magazine. His promises had the ability to make my heart dance, like Ginger Rogers did on a glossy strip of film with Fred Astaire.

"I INN-TEND-TOO ... " His radio voice continued to flood our kitchen. "HEEEER IN THIS FINNNNE TOWN OF HUUUUUTCH ... " He paused, midway through elaborate vows he could not keep, to praise Hutchinson. He spoke of the town's noble courthouse where justice, which all Republicans pursued, always prevailed. He talked of its fine local citizens, who were loyal to their beautiful community and always adherent to its laws.

"Long live Hutch!" he shouted, evoking a swell of applause from the crowd.

I longed to see him standing there at the podium and yearned to examine the Bisconte hotel. I wanted to know the color of its auditorium walls, sniff the scent of podium flowers that surrounded him, and see whether small American flags waved in the hands of his supporters. I thought of Hutch and wondered whether we had driven past this hotel on the dreaded Saturday shopping excursions there with our grandmother Hattie and our grandfather Perry at the wheel of his Packard.

I wished I had paid more attention to this town instead of pouting about another Saturday wasted shopping. I should have looked for the Bisconte hotel as we traveled local streets to Pegues department store. But I had been too busy moping at the prospect of trailing Hattie past store clerks startled at the sight of an apparent alien who flaunted flaming red hair, piles of chunky jewelry, and elbow-length leather gloves.

En route to each of these shopping marathons, Mom, Margo, Andrea and I always had to sit squashed in the Packard's back seat. The car never ventured off Perry's direct route from their house on Marlin Street in Mac to Pegues. Down the flat stretch of road without horizon. By the towering grain elevators. Thirty miles of dulling scenery. Perry would never have considered varying his route. He resembled a homing pigeon in that regard.

Once we arrived in Hutch, his route always took us through the prosperous part of town. So we had never gotten to peer out the back car windows into the area of rundown neighborhoods, whose residents could never afford the finery Pegues' mannequins wore behind glass show windows. Their feather hats and leather heels would never have appeared on the sidewalks of those tired streets of untidy cinder block houses, interspersed between bars and gas stations.

Should Perry have mistakenly detoured us onto one of these lower-class arteries, like East Fourth Street, Hattie would certainly have locked her car door at once. "Lord a'Mercy," she would probably have uttered, a frail hand fluttering over her chest. "It's downright dangerous here, Perry."

But then constant danger lurked everywhere for Hattie. It threatened outside her house whose doors and windows were bolted shut, indoors where imaginary burglars tampered with window shades, and even on the front yard sidewalk where she forbade my sisters and me to play just as she had my father when he was a boy. So certain was Hattie that something lurked near her back yard's forlorn hollyhocks and struggling sedum that she refused to hang laundry there, and dried it in the basement instead.

The "Dangers List" was what I had labeled her constant admonitions about the frightening possibilities of ominous strangers, errant automobiles, suspicious goings-on, and prowling dogs. Only her ignorance of certifiable dangers, the kind that were transpiring regularly on East Fourth Street, kept them off her roster. Had someone advised her of the illegal activities taking place in the Hutch basement at 1329 East Fourth Street next to a liquor store, she might have concocted an "Extreme Dangers List."

She might also have warned my father that Hutch, with that basement of murderous machinations, was not an appropriate setting in which to accept his GOP political post. Most certainly, she would have advised him not to laud all of its citizens as upstanding and fine, considering the evil woman who operated out of that basement.

"Land Sakes," she might have said. "That horrible person could be killing someone in Hutch right as you're giving your acceptance speech."

Yet we had never traveled down East Fourth Street. So how could any of us — my father who was on the cusp of his ascent to political power right there in Hutch, Hattie who was bankrolling her only child's

5

ambitions, my mother who despised politics, and a trio of young daughters being groomed as political assets — have suspected that a woman who lived in this town, a murderess by the name of Annas Brown who butchered fetuses in her basement, was about to be launched on a trajectory that would land at the heart of my father's political career and the soul of our family?

"INNNN CON-KLUUU-SHUN ... " His radio spiel was winding down. He was beginning to spread a layer of hush over his words, which he relished rearranging like children's toy blocks. Margo started clapping her chubby hands.

"You can turn off the radio now, Cynthia. He's almost done," Grandma Ida said. She put Andrea on the floor and then smoothed wrinkles in her wool skirt.

"But I wanta hear more. Dad's not done yet."

"You'll have plenty of time for that." She extended a long slim arm to twist the radio dial. "Lots of chances to hear his speeches. Your father is going to be governor of Kansas before too long. You just wait and see."

"Dad's gonna be guv-ner! Dad's gonna be guv-ner!" Margo yelled. Andrea started clapping again in celebration of she knew not what.

CHAPTER ONE

PECK'S BAD BOY
1949-1950

My father's climb to power as Kansas Young GOP chairman featured all of the drum rolls and overdone pomp with which he embellished all personal achievements.

It officially began with his ceremonial leave-taking from our rambling frame house on Walnut Street in Mac. His destination was Dodge City. Or Dodge, as everyone called the one-time hangout of gun-toting villains. Dodge was hosting the 1949 Young Republicans fifth congressional district meeting at its American Legion clubhouse. It was to be the launching pad for political fame as he intended to announce his candidacy for the state-wide GOP chairmanship. He planned to wow them in a brand new silk suit financed by Hattie.

He posed in our front hall, next to a soaring staircase that passed a stained glass window above a broad landing. We surrounded his lanky, towering frame. Margo danced her ever-restless feet impatiently. Andrea copied with her toddler awkwardness. I stood by and studied him in silent admiration.

Within days of his return from war three years before, I had decided that my someday-husband must be a replica of my father. If I could not have him for myself, I wanted a carbon copy. My clone of a spouse would have to tower over me at six feet, three inches, and gaze at me with enormous eyes glimmering with adoration. His lips would be sort of thick, and always smiling. He would have to exude the same cologne-drenched scent and wear the stylish wardrobe in which my father strutted. If he was all of that, and could learn to call me Darlin,' I would be able to pretend that my husband was my father.

He began his front hall farewell ceremony by embracing my mother and depositing one of his wet and sloppy kisses. "Snooky," he called her, rather than Virginia. He used her real name only when she irked him. Next he trotted out the nicknames somehow conjured for his trio of daughters. Margo was "Snussy Puss," Andrea was "Doodlebug," and I was "Mrs. Tusswagon." When he spoke of us collectively, we were "The Harem."

For whatever reason, he had to make all of his departures from us as grandiose and prolonged as his speeches on political platforms. He was unable to simply say goodbye, and exit. With each elaborate leave-taking came the lyric that measured the extent of our devotion. "I love you. Do you love me, too?" he always said.

After leaving us for Dodge, he would head his Cadillac southwest toward Hutch, then west through the hamlet of Sylvia, over Rattlesnake Creek, and eventually through Macksville before reaching his destination.

* * * * *

As he arrived, the Dodge City Daily Globe was reporting that Senator Andrew Frank Schoeppel, a former Kansas governor from Ness City, planned to attend. This was uplifting news since he had been firmly entrenched in my father's political support base since 1945. That was when he had begun nurturing the contact from aboard his Navy war vessel. From out in the Pacific Ocean, he had summoned the courage to send a letter to Governor Schoeppel, who would lead the Sunflower State until 1947. His composition had contained a personal critique of a Stars and Stripes newspaper article concerning federal officials' involvement in possessing liquor on federal properties. He had slipped some Japanese yen into the envelope as a memorable goodwill gesture.

The governor had nibbled at the bait and responded with a two-page letter typed on "State of Kansas, Officer of the Governor, Topeka" letterhead. My father had pored over that document several times daily ever since, and often recited his favorite part from memory:

"Dear Lieutenant Lackie …

What a pleasure it was to hear from you … I note
that your letter was mailed from Yokosuka, Japan …
I hope to see you back in the States and when you get
back I would be happy if you would stop in. I would
like to talk to you ... Thank you so much for the yen.
I will certainly keep it as a momento … It was nice
of you to write me and I hope that you are back by
Christmas time."

The good news about supporter Schoeppel was tempered by
the unexpected absence of Fred Hall, who was my father's closest political ally. The chairman of the Ford County Young Republican Club,
which included Dodge City, was supposed to preside over the meeting.
But he was ill. Or so the local newspaper reported. Nevertheless, once
in Dodge, candidate Lackie made his chairmanship ambitions widely
known to the rabid Republicans who did attend. Afterward, the <u>Dodge
City</u> <u>Daily</u> <u>Globe</u> heralded his candidacy on its front page, bestowing
all of the homage he expected:

"A high light of the preconvention activities was
formal announcement by Paul Lackie of McPherson as
a candidate for state Young Republican chairman."

He was en route to the political prize, hurtling toward state-wide
power as fast as he could travel.

* * * * *

So now here we were again, just four weeks later, assembled in our
front hall to bid my father adieu. This occasion was far more auspicious
than the Dodge City departure. His political future was at stake down
the road in Hutch. He needed to slaughter a pair of rivals in order to
snare the coveted chairmanship. One was a State Representative by the

9

name of Charles D. Stough. "Go for Stough! He'll blow your dough," he ridiculed. The other, a county attorney from Norton named Keith Sebelius, earned potshots like "Good grief! It's Kuh-EEEth."

He applauded one newspaper that described Stough as "a latecomer who is using standard political snowball tactics to get the chairmanship." Yet this ridiculed Charles Stough would go on to serve as the 1953 Speaker of the Kansas House of Representatives. Keith Sebelius would be elected to the U.S. House of Representatives, and serve from 1969 to 1981.

For a solid month, we had listened to negative pronouncements about Stough and dough, Keith and good grief. We had heard all of their flaws presented in contrast to our resident candidate who had none. He had wooed us daily, as if we would be in Hutch to cast ballots.

"Your name is Mrs. Tusswagon, I believe," he had said, reaching out his hand to grip mine. "Remember me by my initials P.A.L., Paul Andrew Lackie, your pal, the only worthy candidate for state GOP chairman." He had followed one or the other of us all about the house, rehearsing his political views to our retreating backs.

That my father was incapable of doing anything without demanding our full attention did not occur to me as unusual at the time. Fathers were intended to star at the center of their families with everyone else orbiting around them. That was my understanding. A father was to be idolized, not questioned. Otherwise, family life would not proceed smoothly. At least that was the rule in our house.

My mother seemed to accept the reality that her dislike of politicians, and what they represented, did not count. She did manage to make it clear, though, that my father's passion for anything political ranked up there with her intolerance for people who possessed no taste in clothing or home furnishings. "Taste. You can't buy it. Either you've got it, or not," she liked to pronounce.

On occasion, she was able to make her political sentiments clear in small acts of defiance. The most recent one was her refusal to accompany him to the crucial contest in Hutch. She used my sisters and me as her excuse.

"SOMEONE must stay home and rear these girls," she pronounced in the booming voice she could summon for such occasions. "SOMEONE needs to act responsible once in awhile."

Instead of standing obediently at his side in Hutch, she stayed home and read to us about the GOP political proceedings from the newspaper. On the first day, a Friday, she told us that The Hutchinson News-Herald had written:

> "Another skirmish in Kansas' perennial civil war, east vs. west, will be fought here this weekend as Young Republicans and a raft of state GOP leaders gather for a 2-day state convention."

The following day, she read us the paper's rollicking account of those convention festivities:

> "Hutchinson glowed Friday night with a political fervor she hasn't known since the days of Sockless Jerry Simpson. Kansas Young Republicans … were staging the liveliest state convention in recent history. The issues were narrowed Friday night to an all-out political fight, involving Charles Stough of Lawrence, Paul Lackie of McPherson and Keith Sebelius of Norton … The chairmanship situation still was confused. Most delegates agreed that by Saturday noon it would be narrowed to a duel between Stough and Lackie … Elsewhere the convention mostly was hand-shaking and glass-gripping. Conventioneers milled through the Bisconte corridors, greeted fraternity brothers and political soul-mates."

To my "What are soul-mates?" question, she delivered one of her "I am not going to explain that now" looks. She did not go into detail either about how my father must have jockeyed for position to garner votes from big counties like Shawnee, wooing their representatives through walls of thick smoke and pools of flowing booze. Listening to her read, I did not consider the liquor and cigarette part of the article abnormal because my father indulged in both with regularity.

Saturday in Hutch brought the final verdict. My father was no doubt bleary-eyed and hoarse of voice by then as conventioneers cast their ballots. But undoubtedly, he was supremely confident. And sure enough, before the sun set on Saturday night outside the Bisconte hotel, the announcement was made that Paul Andrew Lackie had beaten back his competitors. The charismatic candidate from McPherson had become the newly elected chairman of the Young Republicans of Kansas. He had worked the magic he practiced on my sisters and me, and repelled the forces of Dough and Good Grief.

As the <u>McPherson County News</u> later summarized his coup:

> "Lackie piled up strong backing in late maneuvering … "

Sunday newspapers, state-wide, heralded the results. The <u>Salina Journal</u> was among those proclaiming the elevation of another Republican in a state that coveted them like fine gems:

> "Lackie rolled up 167 votes against 56 for his nearest rival, Keith Sebelius, (Norton), and 25 for Charles D. Stough, state representative from Lawrence."

His enormous eyes peered out at us from a score of newspaper front pages. His professional head shot made him look pensive and overly serious. He stared solemnly with only the hint of a smile, which made his lips part slightly. It was not an expression that was familiar to me. He would have needed to roll his eyes or grin mischievously at the photographer in order to resemble his regular self. But he had said that politicians were supposed to appear contemplative and mature to their constituents. Since he was only 34 years old and had swept rather effortlessly over the first political hurdle in his run for the Kansas governor's seat, maybe he was attempting to communicate credibility.

He phoned our house from Hutch. I heard my mother on the kitchen telephone saying, "That's wonderful, Paul" and "Yes, it must be very exciting." Her usual strung-out diction was even more pronounced than usual. She could never have captured a single voter's support with such an indifferent, but unmistakable, tenor.

Reluctantly, she succumbed to his pleas to join him and attend the post-election political melee in Hutch. After hanging up, she telephoned Grandma Ida to journey from home in nearby Marquette and play baby sitter. "Paul won" is all we heard her tell Grandma Ida.

Then my sisters and I started the wait for the sight of our grandmother's car as eagerly as we would have anticipated ice cream sodas. For me, each of her visits was like an unsought gift. I could never have confided it to anyone. But I considered her companionship preferable to that of Mom.

Exactly what my mother said to us at the time about my father's political plum has been overpowered in memory by the indelible excitement of hearing him speak on the radio. Whether she looked disconsolate, or merely resigned, is a blur. But a souvenir photograph, snapped of them in a Hutch Young Republicans receiving line, has survived that occasion. It shows them posing as a supposedly elated couple. She portrayed the proud wife, an image of elegance in hat and gloves, who stood next to her beaming husband and smiled politely as someone grasped her hand. He looked appropriately dashing, eyeballing the person who was congratulating him with his mouth open as if about to interrupt. One certainty is evident in the photo. Without question, they would have made a stunning governor and first lady of Kansas.

Perhaps that victory was what caused me to jump onto the runaway train of my father's ambitions. It turned him into a bona fide newspaper-picture-and-political-quotes celebrity. All of his ardent claims as a political force to be reckoned with, and his boisterous boasts of future stardom, had been verified. As he rhapsodized about his future, it never occurred to me not to support him. The family fan club had already been launched by Hattie, who intoned "Governor Paul ANNN-drew Lackie" as she gazed at him during our Sunday visits.

Since he referred to all prominent politicians as if they were bosom friends, or at least more than casual acquaintances, I assumed that to be a fact. My friends, whose dads toiled in factories or behind desks, did not orbit in such political auras. So they listened with certain awe as my father dropped names of governors and senators in their presence. Sometimes they asked me later, "Was he talking about OUR governor?" or "Is your father FAMOUS?" I answered the first question affirmatively. In response to the second one, I tried to sound modest while saying, "Yes, I suppose Dad is famous."

Yet I wondered sometimes if my friends would have reacted with such envy if forced to listen constantly to his rhetoric, as in a typical dinner conversation at our house. It went something like, "How about that letter from Frank?" He said it to my mother across the dining room table.

"Frank who?" She busied herself refolding a cloth napkin.

"WHO?" His eyes drifted my way, seeking support. At least she had not uttered her usual "As my father always said, 'Politicians are a bunch of phonies.'"

"GUVVV-UH-NUH Frank Carlson, my friend Frank, governor of this GRAAA-TE state of Kansas, THAT Frank." He winked at me.

I knew about that letter, written on thick creamy paper with the State of Kansas emblem embossed on it. When no one was looking, I had read what Governor Carlson composed:

"Dear Mr. and Mrs. Lackie,

… I was sorry I was unable to attend and have an opportunity to again meet with you … If at any time I, or my office, can be of assistance to you please do not hesitate to call upon me …

Best personal regards."

"Damn shame Frank couldn't make it," my father said, pushing the broccoli he detested about his plate.

Listening to him, I wished he would ask, "What did you do in school today, Cynthia?" On rare occasions, he did. But it was always unexpected. I knew, just as my sisters did, that we were to sit silently during his soliloquies, eating with our right hands and keeping left ones in our laps. We were to chew with our mouths closed, and absolutely never open them in order to interrupt.

"Sit up straight, Margo," my mother admonished as he launched into recollections of the Fourth District Young Republicans convention he had convinced her to attend recently in Topeka.

"At least Freddie made it, even if Frank didn't."

"Freddie, Freddie!"

"Stop it!" My mother glared at Margo, who was forever being punished for her escapades.

Even at five, Margo knew about Fred Hall. All of us did. He was my father's bosom political pal, the one he called Freddie. One future day, my sisters and I would copy and call him that, too. But we would never refer to him as "The Little Man," like newspapers sarcastically depicted him.

What we could not suspect was that Freddie's destiny was to become hitched to ours as surely as was that of abortionist Annas Brown. We had no way of knowing that his image of thick spectacles and short frame, and a personality which would be described as pugnacious and ambitious, were to become emblazoned on our minds and hearts forever.

15

Back then, Freddie was the most legitimate friend in the ranks of my father's political cronies. They included the governor he called Frank, a Democratic president from Missouri referred to as either Harry or "Give-Em-Hell-Harry," his law partner and former Kansas Senator James Cassler whom he called "The Senator," and his all-time hero whose name was Abe.

Freddie's full name was Frederick Lee Hall. He hailed from Dodge City, known among Kansans as much for hideous dust storms as for outlaws. My father was a home-grown "Why would anybody in their right mind want to live anywhere but Mac?" product.

Both hungered for the same political prize. Winning it meant residing in Topeka, sitting in the governor's chair, and determining the fate of all their Kansas subjects.

On respective resumes submitted as qualification to be public servants, they would have emerged as relative equals. Both were lawyers. My father boasted Jayhawk allegiance as a University of Kansas law grad. Freddie claimed the University of Southern California, which he had attended as a political science major on a four-year National High School Achievement Scholarship. In 1941, he had graduated from its law school. Each possessed a silver tongue, having excelled in school debate. Freddie had even been a member of the U.S.C. International Debate Team. Ironically, both of their fathers worked in railroad jobs. That was a fact neither dwelled on as a political asset.

As for military service, my father offered a slightly more patriotic edge. Along with a bumper crop of other proud Kansans, he had marched off to World War II and become a Navy Amphibious Forces Lieutenant. Though he had hardly been a model physical specimen, apparently Freddie had been even less fit. He failed his military physical examination and had to take a desk job, as assistant director of the Combined Production and Resource Board for the Combined Chiefs of Staff in Washington, D.C., from 1942 to 1944. War's end brought them back to Kansas. Freddie had headed to Topeka to toil for two years at a law firm until his home town beckoned. Back in Dodge, he had served as the County Attorney for Ford County until defeat for a second term propelled him into private law practice. My father had made a beeline directly back to Mac and rejoined his law practice with The Senator.

Of all the similarities between this power-hungry pair, their passion for Republican politics was the glue that bound them. It was almost as if the almighty ruling gods of politics had blueprinted a plan for these two to converge and take turns leading the Sunflower State. The deities' scheme did not require them to tread identical paths though.

Now their routes were about to fork off into distinctly divergent directions. Freddie had hatched an ambitious plan to get him to the governor's mansion first. He intended to leapfrog past my father and run for Kansas lieutenant governor in 1950. It was a risky move, considering that eight other Republicans also intended to seek the office.

Such gambling instincts were another common denominator Paul Andrew Lackie and Frederick Lee Hall shared. Each had a very high tolerance for risk.

* * * * *

Freddie, Frank, Give-Em-Hell-Harry, The Senator, Abe, and all the other politicians we heard about incessantly during my father's political monologues shared prominence in his mind with Civil War heroes.

One was General James Birdseye McPherson, the namesake of our town. It infuriated him that they had honored this particular veteran instead of someone else. "Why the hell did they name Mac after a Commander of the Army of Tennessee?" He confronted me, frequently, with this inquiry about the war hero who had been born in Ohio and died in the 1864 Battle of Atlanta.

At 10, I did not even attempt to answer the inquiry presented during our Saturday afternoon motor trips together around Mac. It baffled me why he was compelled to rant about the sanity of the town found-

17

ers, and why they failed to name it after someone like General George Armstrong Custer. I had never heard anyone else's father carry on as mine did about decisions made by people they had never even met. Sometimes I toyed with the idea of diverting him and offering other famous names they might have considered as candidates, like Abraham Lincoln or George Washington. But George had gotten nabbed by Easterners. And Abe had been singled out by Nebraska. Besides, bringing up Lincoln would only have precipitated another monologue about his favorite politician. So I just nodded my head once in awhile and looked at him as he railed, "Custer at least traveled the Santa Fe trail outside town. General Mac never even set foot here. South Dakota was smart enough to honor Custer. Why the hell not Kansas?"

Our Saturday auto tours of Mac departed from our garage, next to a concrete alley where my sisters, the neighborhood kids and I chased one another or hid. "Would you like to ride in my beautiful balloon?" my father crooned en route to the garage.

He seemed to regard his shiny Cadillac as a personal appendage. His eyes shone while easing his long frame behind the wheel of a vehicle my mother insisted we could not afford. Sometimes he talked to it, softly, as if to a beautiful female who had stolen his breath.

For some reason, one particular tour lingers in my memory. It began, like most of them, with a detour past the regal home of his law partner, The Senator. He and his elegant wife lived in a sprawling red brick house, with a fish pond next to its circle drive. It was catty-corner behind ours. She was a Southern general's daughter my father said each time we passed by. "Damned if those Confederates don't still think they won the war, Southern so-and-so's. Wrong side of the war Abe oversaw so nobly." The Senator's wife was a "real looker" though, he always added. It delegated her to the upper echelons of his rank ordering of females' beauty, the "real babe" or "quite a dame" category. At least she did not merit his "older than the mother of God" or "She could haunt a house" designation.

18

The rest of our neighbors resembled a closet of mismatched shoes, all tossed together in one pile. Next door to the refined Casslers lived Wilbur Mackie, who drove a tired pickup and brought home glass bottles of thick cream from his dairy. "Rub-a-dub-dub, all the Mackies equal a tub," my father said at the sight of him waddling out to his truck. The neighborly hodgepodge also featured a doctor living across the street from a piano teacher, who lived next door to a factory worker, who shared the sidewalk with a clothing store owner.

One thing our neighbors did have in common was that all of them considered my father odd. It was not just because of his fancy clothes and ostentatious automobile in a neighborhood of mostly Chevys and Fords. It was more due to the fact that he never ventured outdoors to join their "How's the crabgrass problem?" or "Got a new mower?" conversations. He was never outside at all, except to traverse our back sidewalk from house to garage.

He had hired George-the-Gardener to tend our weeds and rake leaves alongside the neighbors. We could not be sure of the origin of George, who arrived daily in a battered truck and never talked to any of us. "Owes me some money, George does," was all my father would say about the modest man with tiny eyeglasses, who wore overalls and a straw hat.

"What kind of politician spends Saturdays laboring out in his yard anyway?" he asked us. "Can you imagine the governor of Kansas having to clean up the Capitol grounds?"

A dozen or so blocks away from home, our motor tour arrived uptown in front of an imposing bronze statue of General McPherson astride his horse. It sat in Memorial Park, site of the native limestone courthouse. My father always insisted that we pause there in honor of the Civil War veterans. He glanced at the general and his horse before turning his attention to a big plaque. He read its inscription out loud:

"McPherson County Roll of Honor 1861-1865.
The world can never forget what they did."

"Mrs. Tusswagon, now those were real patriots," he said, reaching over to squeeze my knee. "Just look at the 752 names on that plaque, those brave men who died in places like Appomattox and Gettysburg. You know, Abe ... "

That sent him into a reverie about the man from Illinois, with whom he claimed to have so much in common. Grandmothers born in Kentucky. Grandfathers reared on Illinois farms. Both of them attorneys. And Republicans, of course. On occasion, he even quoted from one of Abe's speeches. Inevitably, he wove tales of his own supposed Navy derring-do with Civil War heroics until they, he, and Abe fit together seamlessly. No war was easy, he reminded me, be it Civil or the one in which he had participated.

* * * * *

It made me think of that frigid January day in 1946 when he had come back to us from the war and our first sight of him at Mac's Chicago, Rock Island & Gulf Railway station. My grandfather Perry was its ticket master then.

Our little family had clustered on the platform, bursting with excitement. Hattie had even ventured out of her house for the homecoming. That meant it had to be an extra special occasion. The fur collar on her wool coat had moved in the raw wind. Her anxious face, arrested in grief since his departure nearly five years before, had looked suddenly softer. Focusing on the train tracks, she had stared as if that could produce her Paul Andrew. My mother had stood near me, wrestling with the energetic bundle that was my sister Margo. She was one month shy of a year old, and my father had only seen her in photographs. Margo was a product of the trip my mother and I had made to California to visit his Navy base.

My mother had been enchanted with the palm trees and sunshine, and begged my father to resettle them there.

"Lord a'Mercy," Hattie had uttered with a sickly swoon. Why, Mac was the only place Paul Andrew had ever belonged. She had glanced defiantly toward my mother.

Our wait for the train was beginning to seem interminable when, suddenly, we had heard a screaming whistle in the distance. The train had come racing down the tracks toward us and then screeched to a stop. We had looked frantically from one car door to another.

All at once, there he had stood. He was stiff and starched in Navy whites, and framed in the open door of the railroad car in front of us. He had posed as if awaiting flashbulbs or political interviews to commence. Then he had descended the steps, one long leg, then the other. He was as slender as the January icicles suspended from trees near the station. He had winked down at me, eyes flashing their flirtatious blue beneath the military hat tipped smartly above them.

"Oh, my darling Paul Andrew," murmured Hattie, sagging.

I had glanced at my mother just as a wrinkle of disgust creased her forehead. Her insistence on calling my father Paul, and deleting Andrew which honored Hattie's late father, seemed to wound my grandmother irretrievably.

Once he was on the platform, I had rushed into his knees and held on tight. Reaching down to squeeze my cheek between two fingers, he had said, "I love you, my Mrs. Tusswagon. Do you love me, too?" His breath had floated before him on frigid air.

"Oh yes." My five-year-old heart had felt swollen. I had considered it impossible to love someone more than I did him. For so many nights in bed, I had closed my eyes tight and summoned his image standing before me like this. I had pretended that I stood on this train platform all alone, a welcoming committee of one. In my reveries, the glass marbles that were his eyes had opened wider to make them seem to bob in pools of chalky white. Then he had lifted me, murmuring one of the gooey endearments that had been scribbled to me on tissue paper letters from Japan. He had hugged me close, and my heart had begun to dance fancy pirouettes.

21

Margo had started to wail, afraid of this stranger who was trying to kiss our mother. And Hattie's pout had become exaggerated by the time my father wrapped his long arms about her. "I love you. Do you love me, too?" he had asked, rocking her gently.

"I baked your favorite cherry pie, Paul Andrew." She had batted her beady eyes, framed by an enormous hat trimmed in feathers.

My mother's voice had matched the wintry chill. "Hattie, maybe we should go to our house instead."

Hattie had examined her with flat eyes, then turned toward my father. Her thin lips had trembled slightly.

"Mama, we'll come just for a bit." His eyeballs had skidded past my mother's frigid face which had donned one of her fury masks.

* * * * *

I was still thinking about that homecoming day as he slowed our auto tour to a crawl from a pace that already felt like navigating through thick oil. "There it is, Mrs. Tusswagon," he said. We were on Chestnut Street, a block from General Mac on his horse. An elegant Southern plantation style house, complete with fat porch pillars and a porte-cochere to one side, sat on the corner. He always included it on our motor tours. A sign out front identified it as a repository for corpses. It caused him to begin relating a story that intrigued me far more than dead Civil War fighters.

"I was born in that funeral home, you know," he started. "Maybe that's why they nicknamed me 'Peck's Baaa-d Boy.'" He inhaled his Pall Mall, then peered at me for reaction. "What does that mean, Peck?" I asked each time, hopeful that just once he would offer an informative response.

Instead he rambled off into allusions to Peter Piper and his peck of pickled peppers. He failed to include the fact that the wife of Woodrow Wilson had supposedly tolerated her husband's dalliances with a woman named Mary Peck. Afterward, the naughty president had been nicknamed "Peck's Bad Boy."

Usually, he added sketchy details about this house that Hattie's Swedish parents had owned on that momentous May day when he entered the world. He had come squalling into it in a funeral home room that was dark with heavy woodwork and drawn draperies. No one had thought Hattie could ever have children. So he had begun life as a bona fide miracle. "Maybe that's why she calls me 'My World's Dearest Treasure,'" he said, puffing with self-importance.

Hard as I tried, I could not imagine my frail and sickly grandmother giving birth to any baby. I could only envision her as she appeared during our Sunday visits, sitting on her stool in the kitchen corner with socks rolled at her ankles.

Through my childhood and beyond, I would carry that same image of her. She was positioned next to a white metal medicine cabinet in a faded plaid house dress, terry-cloth slippers on feet crossed one over the other, bright red hair awry in home-permed ringlets, head tilted to stare at the drab linoleum, and knotted hands bulging with ripples of blue veins. Thin, chalky white skin stretched like fragile parchment across her bony nose, around bullet-shape dark eyes, and past the sad mouth. She appeared to be on the verge of one of her "Spells," those mysterious incidents of heart palpitations and possible swoons which threatened to take her "into the beyond." Once I dreamt about squeezing Hattie's hands so hard that liquid, like dark blue ink, spurted from her corner and dripped off the cast iron stove.

Armed with those impressions of my grandmother, it seemed beyond my comprehension to picture her with the swollen abdomen my friends' pregnant mothers developed. Or lying in that dark and deathly house producing my father from between her skinny legs.

After the funeral home, we headed uptown to pass by the Cassler and Lackie law firm sign. This caused my father to wax into a soliloquy about his prestigious partner. As far as I was able to tell, he would have preferred to have someone like The Senator as his father instead of Perry. "The Senator thinks of me as the son he never had," he often said to my mother.

Maybe he believed that had fortune made him a child of the Casslers, his life might have been more grand. He would have grown up with a full-time maid like theirs who made cucumber sandwiches and ironed napkins, might have attended an Eastern university instead of lowly McPherson College, and could have picked up coeds in his spiffy auto instead of a beater Chevy. Perhaps our recent move into the grand dame of a house near the Casslers had been a calculated way to solidify that connection.

* * * * *

Our home before Walnut Street had been a small frame house on a corner one block off Main Street. What remains now of the memories I formed by the time we left it is oddly selective. They consist of a front-porch awning with broad green and white stripes, and the living room. I can still picture its chairs of rich silk stripes, and matching tassel-trimmed lamps. Particularly memorable is the floral sofa, with fabric so realistic that people sitting on it appeared to be surrounded by an opulent flower garden.

Mainly what I remember about that house with the striped umbrella-like entry is my parents' big fight. It had begun immediately after my mother closed my bedroom door when the nightly "Now I lay me down to sleep. I ... " prayer was finished.

She had launched the first grenade. He had no right to withdraw her inheritance money from the bank without asking, she had screeched. It was HERS! "My father left it to me, NOT you," she had ranted. It was no different from stealing, and only a thief would go behind your back and take money that belonged to someone else.

His responding voice had sounded gravely wounded, as if someone were throwing darts at him. He called her "Snooky," and promised he

24

had meant no harm. He had done it only because she wanted to own that house on Walnut Street, more than anything he could remember her ever desiring. Anyway, where the hell else was the down payment supposed to come from?

I had tiptoed across my bedroom carpet and cracked open the door. I had never heard my father yell. Only my mother did that.

"My father warned me not to marry you," she had railed. Her voice had seeped hatred as she directed a barrage of accusations about untrustworthiness and deception at him. It had made me worry that she might make him go away from us again like he did to war.

* * * * *

Perry declared that our big Walnut Street house was extravagant. My father ignored him as usual, wandering down one of his zigzag verbal trails of money talk that led nowhere.

My suspicion was that he liked this imposing house because it was the sort that would cause Mac residents, passing by in cars or on the sidewalk, to issue compliments. They would be apt to smile at the sight of those adorable daughters of that upcoming politician playing there on a sweep of emerald green lawn. Of course, they would not be able to peek into the house's commodious rooms, which all needed renovation. So they probably thought instead that all of the rooms were glamorous, as they soon would be. Transforming them to grandeur was the kind of magic my mother could easily perform. Needy though it might be, she had been enthralled with that house at first sight. If it was possible to conduct a love affair with an inanimate object, she was doing so.

* * * * *

The final stop on our Saturday tour of Mac was "Tank Up Time." My father announced it while threading down Main Street, past angle-parked pickups with dogs pacing their open backs, by storefronts whose

25

signs identified owners like Odell's Help-Self Laundry or Crabb's Town and Country, past local snoops whose daily activities consisted of monitoring passers-by from street benches, and up to North Main and Harry B. Dorst American Legion Post No. 24.

En route, he offered me confidences concerning local goings-on. "Jones is going to develop that property." He pointed to a vacant store. "His wife inherited a bundle, Texas oil, you know." He strayed off into a verbal mishmash of speculation. "Just between you and me, Mrs. Tusswagon, I'm thinkin' of investing in an Oklahoma well myself. Now don't mention that to your mother. It'll be our lil' secret."

Finally, he pulled up in front of the square brick box of a building that housed the American Legion and said, "In we go, Mrs. Tusswagon." We encountered a thick haze of cigarette smoke even before entering the dim cave of a room filled with raucous voices and clinking ice cubes. Behind the bar, a man in a Legion cap grabbed bottles of whiskey or vodka that seemed to be hidden somewhere near the floor. He poured from them into glasses held out for him.

"The usual, Dusty," my father said, hoisting me onto a tall stool at the bar. "My best girl here, Mrs. Tusswagon, will have a Shirley Temple. She's part of The Harem back home, ya know." He yanked gently at a pigtail my mother had braided and ornamented with a grosgrain ribbon, then reached for a full glass of vodka. "Isn't she a looker with those big eyes and dark hair?"

Leaving me stranded on the stool, he maneuvered to the center of the crowd. Along the way, he paused to draw fellow Legionnaires to his side. He tossed out political tidbits as lures to make them circle about him. "NOWWW ... " he began, imploring silence for his current political observations. He reminded them of world tribulations and carried on about "those goddamned Oriental SOBs, who had the nerve to bomb Pearl Harbor." He derided the Democrats and their inept leader "Franklunn Dell-uh-NOOO ROOO-suh-VELLLt," as he called him.

By then, he had their full attention. For Mac was a town where patriotism did not need to be imposed. It was already rooted firmly in most local hearts. Residents expected one another to fly American flags daily. They rippled like tri-color paintings along Main Street and through leafy neighborhoods. It seemed like every day in Mac was Flag Day, not just June 14th.

Dusty eyed me sympathetically and poured another Shirley Temple as my father waxed on about the state budget, those Demo no-goods, national political shenanigans, on and on. Liquid refills from bottles furnished by Legion members, due to "dry as a bone" Kansas alcohol laws, fueled the dialogue. I squirmed, my eyes pink from smoke, and awaited my father's predictable wind-up.

Finally, it came. "Boys, you have heard me say it before. I innn-tend tuuuh be GUVVV-UH-NUH UF THIS GRAAA-TE STAAA-TE UF KANNN-SUS. And I'll need your vote. You can count on me."

Back in the Cadillac, he solicited my evaluation of his political remarks. "What'd ya think, Mrs. Tusswagon? Did the boys like it?"

"I ... "

"They've asked me to preside over the Legion flag raising on Memorial Day in the Mac cemetery." He looked sideways at me. "I PUH-LEDDD-JUH ... " he began. "Quite an honor if I do say so myself. Couple of weeks from now, there I'll be, leading the Pledge, right after your mother's birthday. Speaking of that, please don't mention the drinks at the Legion, okay, Mrs. Tusswagon?"

As we neared Walnut Street, he inevitably bestowed Perry's time-worn blessing on Mac. Waving his hand toward some vague landmark, he said, "Why would anybody in their right mind want to live anywhere but Mac?"

* * * * *

My mother, Virginia Mae Teichgraeber Lackie, was about to celebrate her 35th birthday. Unfortunately, our family was usually weary

27

of such celebrations by the time her milestone arrived on May 26th. For if astrological theories prevailed, our family could have been characterized as a posse of stubborn Bulls charging about under the sign of Taurus.

The first Bull of the Month, on May eighth, was my father. The occasion of his birth called for dual family celebrations. Hattie staged an annual culinary tour de force in his honor at her groaning dining room table. She spent days at the stove and produced both his favorite cherry pie and a cake frosted half-vanilla and half-chocolate for dessert. Somehow, we also had to fit in his steak-and-potatoes birthday dinner later in our own dining room.

The following day, the ninth, was my turn as celebrity Bull. Since Hattie executed an extravaganza for her Dearest Treasure but never me, my mother made up for the slight by hosting a party for my friends.

Perry also got honored in late May. His muted observance was highlighted by our annual gift of a cardigan sweater to replace the only one he wore, which was holey. He always acted pleased about our choice. But before the day was over, he placed the new one in a dresser drawer stacked with unworn replicas from a string of birthdays.

Hattie got the same annual birthday gift, too. It was a ribbon-bound packet of handkerchiefs, since she always wore one tucked beneath a rolled-up sleeve. Though we debated and agonized, no one could think what else to give someone who had no hobbies, never read, bought too many clothes, and would never allow flowers in her house in case they bore germs.

Mother's Day called for more May celebrations. I hid in my room, penning verses and drawing hearts on construction paper cards to give Mom, Hattie and Grandma Ida.

My father summed up all of these galas by saying, "Too damned many things to celebrate in May." He despised holidays. They made him more fidgety than usual, devoid of places to flee and at a loss to stay home for an entire day with his family. Inevitably, they also implied conflict concerning mandatory visits to the house on Marlin Street and Grandma Ida in Marquette. No matter the resolution, Hattie would manage to feel wounded.

May also brought the mysterious floating date of my parents' wedding anniversary, with its dubious details.

"When was it?" I asked early each May as the calendar of celebrations began to unfold. Inevitably, my father flipped a hand toward some destination out in space that only he could see and launched into a monologue. My mother responded with one of her multitudinous "Don't bother me with that now" tactics.

I searched the house for a photo album to show their ardent newlywed faces, or to learn whether anyone but them had attended the ceremony. I fished for silly anecdotes about how they had met, or fond tidbits about their courtship. But it proved futile.

They would only admit to having eloped in Lawrence, where my father had been about to enter his final year of law school. Neither ever mentioned an alternate wedding site like a Nebraska town named Fall City, which was across the state line from Kansas. Coincidentally, it was located near the detested post-college, pre-marriage job my mother had as a teacher of high school home economics. Her students had been lackluster girls, mainly programmed to become rural wives and cook smorgasbords for farm hands, she told us once in awhile. But she never described the worst part of that job near the true site of her Nebraska nuptials. That was having to live a solitary life in one rented room of a spinster's house in a town she still referred to as "Hell."

My parents never divulged any details of their first meeting at a Mac dance either. I only found out they had met there when my mother's sister referred to it once. Afterward, I tried to picture it. I wondered whether my mother had worn a sexy slip of a dress, like the lavender one hanging behind other clothes in her closet. I figured that my father had probably blurted details of his political ambitions while mauling her toes with his big feet.

29

Their first love nest of an apartment, above a Lawrence radio station blasting away, remained their private memory, too. It was as if they had forged a pact to treat their pairing and its circumstances as a blank slate, much as they did their childhoods.

As time went on, what would puzzle me more than the secret wedding was the political part. If my mother had known of his intentions ahead of time, why had she gone along on his ride? But then I would think of how convincing he could be, and know the answer.

Though I did not realize it at the time, Mom was at the height of her considerable elegance in her 35th year. She was not runway-model beautiful. Not tall and willowy either, though she was exceedingly slim. Something about her caused total strangers to stare at her anyway. Maybe it was her impeccable posture, refined over years of balancing books on her head as a kid to achieve it. Or her shapely legs, which she accentuated with silk stockings and my father called "those Teichgraeber gams." Or perhaps her aloofness drew attention. People she did not know must have been intrigued with that flip of her lush chocolate hair, the brooding look in her black eyes, and that pouting shape of bright red lips. I suspected that she secretly liked all of this attention while pretending not to notice.

On the rare occasions when she spoke of her past, she described herself as a chubby child and an acne-plagued adolescent. She did not reveal her reputation as a daredevil and cutup, that culprit who had put rocks in her brother's school lunch pail and clowned with a broad smile in teen-age photos. And, of course, she failed to confide that she had been expelled from her college sorority for drinking on its premises, and been nicknamed "Trampy."

These descriptions of daring and humor baffled me. I tried to imagine her acting silly and reckless, or breaking the rules of her sorority. The single photo I had seen of her college days showed Mom in a lush fur coat. She was surrounded by sorority sisters and had thrown back her head in hearty laughter. That person bore no resemblance to the mother I knew.

Most everyone in Mac seemed to like and admire her. She had a host of friends and sallied out with them to play bridge or to their Sewing Club, where they darned socks. But her public smiles turned to frowns inside our house. I knew she did not mean to, but Mom frightened me sometimes. She tended to alternate yelling with profound silences. I did not know how to respond to "the Teichgraeber temper," as my father had labeled the fury that turned her face deep red and her body rigid as a slice of granite. Rage flowed out of her like hot lava, thickening as it accelerated.

I almost preferred that, though, to her silent withdrawal into a private place where none of us could follow. Sometimes I imagined that she retreated there to commune with something secret, which sat shrouded like a mummy at the center of her silence. She had perfected a technique of communicating this state of mind by assuming a frozen face and a look in her eyes that signaled "That's enough." My father called it her "cold shoulder," this muteness that was compressed in layers of ominous silence.

Either of her moods caused him to rotate his eyes my way and assume a hangdog look. He might as well have said out loud, "Oh, Mrs. Tusswagon, what did we do to deserve this?" He looked forlorn, like a child denied a kiss by his mother. But he refused to let her mercurial disposition affect his good nature, and employed jokes to dance around it.

I envied his nonchalance. But emulating him did not work for me. I longed to please her and escape the wounding anger and muteness. She would not have frightened me if she had been able to return to that flippant and fun-loving personality of her youth. But glimpses of that were so rare that I decided to focus on being perfect in hopes of earning her approval.

This 35th birthday of hers seemed extra special. So I came up with the idea of trying to copy her tradition of letting each of us choose our favorite dinner menu. My father invariably ordered steak. I always requested her renowned veal birds. Yet I had no idea what dishes she

31

might have selected. So I settled on meat loaf, which she seemed to like, even though my father detested it.

My mother's best friend, also named Virginia, volunteered to help. For several days before the big evening, I sneaked across the street to her house. She showed me how to mix ground beef with pork, bread crumbs, an egg, an onion, and the rest. On the night of May 26th, she was to bake it in her oven and ferry it to our dining room.

Every day, I fretted about how the party would materialize. I worried that it could be ruined by my father failing to show up for dinner, or their having one of their arguments about politics or drinking. I had not let him in on the surprise for fear that he might tell her by mistake. Anyway, he would have been no help with the preparations. I had never observed him assisting with a single household task, even in the kitchen. His sole concession to acting like a helper was to wear his "Wine, Women and Song" apron.

* * * * *

Around five o'clock on May 26th, as I was setting my mother's walnut dining room table and trying to arrange silverware properly, a young woman was driving down a strip of Kansas road. It connected her home in a southwestern town named Pratt with Hutch. This traveler had no celebration to look forward to as my mother did. She had even bypassed a company party at her workplace to make the trip. She did not have time to eat dinner this night either. Anyway, the thought of downing food would probably have made her more nervous than she already was.

As she traveled, hints of spring dusk were descending on an evening of the sweetest season the Sunflower State offered. It was a time of bursting yellow forsythia, red tulips, white jonquils, and purple lilacs that sent forth a symphony of scents. Alone in her car, with emotions tugging at her edges, this woman was hardly apt to notice the velvety air that would soon summon fireflies to flit their golden lanterns. The somber mission bringing her from Pratt to Hutch was too preoccupying to allow thoughts of flowers and insects.

Joy Malee Joy, 25 years old, was five months pregnant with an unwanted fetus. The divorced linotype operator, mother of six-year-old Vicki, was determined to destroy it. This desperate young woman had no way of knowing that she was about to suffer the same fate.

CHAPTER TWO

MURDER IN THE BASEMENT
1955

When Joy Malee Joy arrived in Hutch, she directed her car toward East Fourth Street. She slowed down at the sight of house number 1329. A gas station sat across from this modest cinder block home. She pulled into its entry.

The station attendant watched through a window as the brunette driver, barely five feet tall and just over 100 pounds, got out and entered his place. He eyed her blue slacks and white blouse as she asked to use his telephone. After she finished dialing, R. T. Davis eavesdropped. He never suspected that an attorney in a courtroom would someday ask him to recreate what she said: "I'll be right over." She hung up the receiver, returned to her car, drove it across the street, parked at the curb, went up the sidewalk and knocked on the door at 1329 East Fourth Street. It was approximately 6:30.

The woman who opened the door of the cinder block house was Annas Whitlow Brown. She was a 25-year resident of Hutch, the mother of two adult daughters, the ex-wife of John S. Brown who operated the liquor store next door, and an untrained abortionist.

Mrs. Brown, as newspapers would refer to her, conducted her so-called "treatments" in the basement of her home. To carry out those abortions, she wore a light bulb strapped to her head as a coal miner might. It provided light while she inserted a duckbill shaped utensil into a pregnant woman's uterus. Dried particles of skin adhered to that abortion tool quite frequently.

Originally, Joy Malee Joy was to have visited Mrs. Brown two weeks before. But for some reason she had rescheduled their rendezvous. Despite suffering from a severe cold, she had decided to keep this appointment. She would have been able to obtain a legal abortion in Kansas only if her life were threatened physically by the prospect of giving birth. Otherwise, she needed the medical recommendation of a physician to get rid of her fetus.

Exactly what transpired in the basement at 1329 East Fourth Street after the young woman entered it at 6:30 would be embellished afterward with contradictory details. Yet the conclusion was tragic and undeniable. Joy Malee Joy, whom R. T. Davis would later describe as having looked "hale and hearty," would be pronounced dead just over an hour later.

At 7:25, the Johnson and Sons funeral home in Hutch received a frantic phone call from Annas Brown. She wanted an ambulance sent to her house, immediately.

Phil Johnson, the funeral home owner, rushed to the address which also belonged to John S. Brown's liquor store. He was sent to the residence next door. Mrs. Brown led the ambulance driver through her garage to the basement. There Phil Johnson encountered the gruesome sight of a young woman lying on a large bed in "a wide spot of blood" as he later described it. He concluded that the victim, whose blouse was unbuttoned down its front, was unconscious and possibly dead.

Annas Brown claimed that the "little girl," as she called her patient, was a stranger who had visited the next-door liquor store to use its bathroom. But John S. Brown's store had no toilet facilities. So Mrs. Brown had generously offered to let Joy Malee Joy use hers.

Phil Johnson transported the victim to his ambulance, and raced her to Grace Hospital. Somewhere en route, or maybe back in the abortionist's basement, the wounded woman died.

At the hospital, Dr. C. W. Haines pronounced her dead. The physician, from Haven, just happened to be there at the time "tending to his patients."

An hour and a half later, around nine o'clock, Annas Brown opened her front door to a pair of Hutch police officers. Detective John Robinson and Deputy Sheriff Gene Schroder inquired whether they could enter to ask her some questions, and tour the house.

Inside, she led the officers to a first-floor bedroom and told her version of the story. It was that the victim could not possibly have died at her hands during an abortion. She had never even met the "little girl" until happening to encounter her on the sidewalk in front of her house. The poor thing needed a bathroom and asked if she could use hers, said Annas Brown. The "little girl" got sick while using the toilet, she told the policemen. So she placed her on the bed. When Joy Malee Joy suffered a "coughing spell," the abortionist furnished a peppermint and a glass of water. Then when she fainted, Annas Brown tried to revive her. When that did not work, she called an ambulance.

When the officers informed the abortionist that they did not believe her story, she led them to the basement. There they noticed a partially-washed bedspread hanging in the utility room. They also saw a second bedspread in a hall that appeared to have been completely washed. Of it, Detective Robinson would later say: "She told me she had washed the one in the hall that morning. I felt of it and knew otherwise."

She did not explain to them why 55 minutes had elapsed between the victim's arrival and the ambulance call. Or why Joy Malee Joy was found in the basement instead of upstairs on a bed. She also failed to say that her victim had turned blue as a result of the botched abortion.

Officers Robinson and Schroeder remained at the house for some time and kept their questions flowing.

At one point, the abortionist said to them: "Do I look like the kind of woman who gets excited?" They ignored her.

Then finally, Annas Brown broke. "I lied," she admitted.

That was hardly a surprise to the visiting officers. As Detective Robinson would later quip: "She admitted she storied us."

The following day, Saturday, a flurry of activity ensued with the goal of organizing a coroner's jury to assess brutal events of the night before. It took all day to summon six men, who would comprise an impromptu jury, and nine witnesses.

By evening, they were ready and convened at the Johnson and Sons funeral home. For two-and-one-half hours, the jury would listen to testimony about the botched abortion. Afterward, it would take them just 15 minutes to determine Annas Brown's fate.

The murderess, who newspapers would later describe as "portly" and "matronly," chose not to dress formally for the proceedings regarding her crime. She showed up wearing a brown cotton dress and sandals, with her hair in braids. She arrived in a 1950 Cadillac, accompanied by her daughter Juanita Whitlow.

The Browns had hired Attorney Don Shaffer to defend the abortionist. Representing the prosecution was Reno County Attorney John Fontron. Judge E. Victor Wilson had been chosen to oversee the night's events.

It began with testimony of two physicians, who had performed the Joy autopsy. Dr. L. C. Murphy, a pathologist, cited "two findings."

"First, the examination showed a five months pregnancy," he said. "Second, there was evidence of instrumentation. There was evidence of an attempt at an abortion."

Dr. Murphy noted that death could have resulted from either loss of blood or from asphyxiation. Vomiting had taken place and resulted in a blockage of the throat, he added. The victim's severe cold could have been a contributing factor, he suggested. "An acute cold, coughing, could have resulted in death if weakened by anesthetic or loss of blood."

The abortion had never been completed, only started, theorized the doctor. That had initiated a "heavy flow of blood," he said. "There was no way to tell how much loss of blood was suffered."

Dr. G. A. Chickering, a coroner, agreed with Dr. Murphy's findings. His additional observation was: "In my opinion, death was caused by an operation or the circumstances surrounding it."

Annas Brown's colleague in crime, a registered nurse with 35 years' experience named Margaret Dowdy, filled the jury in on her role in assisting the abortionist. She also offered them specifics of the night Joy Malee Joy died.

37

It was customary for Annas Brown to refer clients to Nurse Dowdy following their "treatments," she said. Typically, the abortionist identified incoming clients by their home town. So the murder victim was known to Nurse Dowdy only as "the girl from Pratt," she said. The only other information Annas Brown had offered was that the victim had a daughter who lived in Cunninngham with her grandmother. "I never heard of Joy Malee Joy," said Nurse Dowdy.

Annas Brown had phoned Nurse Dowdy the night of the murder to say that "the little girl from Pratt" would be arriving that evening to stay with her. "She called again in a few minutes, about 15 minutes, and said the girl was sick and had turned blue and would I come right out," recalled Nurse Dowdy.

By the time she arrived at the Brown residence, the victim had been rushed away by ambulance. Nurse Dowdy proceeded to the basement, which she described as having two bedrooms, a utility room, and a bath. There she encountered Annas Brown.

"She (Brown) told me the girl asked to use the bathroom, had a severe coughing spell and then asked to lie down on the bed again. She gasped a few times and was gone. There was a large red spot on the bed."

County Attorney Fontron asked: "Do you know what the girl was there for?"

"Not definite, but I had an idea."

"Did you form an opinion?"

"Yes."

"What was it?"

"To have an abortion, I imagine."

"Have you been to the Brown house before?"

"Yes."

"Do they use instruments?"

"All doctors do. I never saw her use any."

"Have you had patients of hers before?"

"Yes."

"Are you an abortionist?"

"Oh, no. I've never done an abortion. I just do the cleaning up, the after care."

"Patients usually stay three or four days?"

"Yes," said Nurse Dowdy. "I keep them in bed and feed them. I determine when they are ready to go."

"Do they pay you?"

"Yes. They pay her (Brown) for her part and me for mine."

"How much do you charge for three or four days?"

"Ten dollars a day." (about $75 today)

One of the jurors interjected a question: "Do you give them any medicine?"

"Just aspirin and laxatives," Nurse Dowdy replied.

The cross-examination continued: "In case they get sick do you call a doctor?"

"I've never had that happen."

The victim was identified after the murder by items in her purse. Prominent among its contents was a business card listing Annas Brown and her telephone number. Scribbled in pencil on its back was Nurse Dowdy's name, address, and phone.

Asked about the card, the nurse admitted having "seen cards like that before."

And to whom were such cards given? "Oh, friends, acquaintances, people," she said.

A month before her fatal abortion, Joy Malee Joy had approached Frank Arnnett, a friend from Pratt, and "intimated she was pregnant." County Attorney Fontron asked him: "Did she say anything about an abortion?"

"No," Arnnett said.

A week after that incident, the victim approached Arnnett again and asked to borrow money.

Arnnett was not the only one who was unaware that Joy Malee Joy was pregnant. So was her mother. Mrs. Lewis, weeping on the witness stand, said that her daughter had fibbed about her plans for the fatal night. She told her mother that she was going to a friend's shower, and would be late getting home that evening. Mrs. Lewis said that her daughter's alleged cold had been severe but "was better Friday."

Grace Hospital night supervisor Martha Fritzmeier was the final witness. Then the coroner's jury left to confer. Apparently, their minds were already made up. Fifteen minutes later, they announced a decision. It was that: (Joy Malee Joy) "came to her death as a result of complications arising from an attempted abortion by person or persons unknown."

Annas Whitlow Brown was charged with first-degree manslaughter. She entered no plea.

Judge Wilson set her bond at $7,500. County Attorney Fontron lobbied for the amount to be increased to $10,000. But the judge prevailed. The abortionist paid her $7,500 (about $56,000 today) and departed in her Cadillac. She was due back in court for a preliminary hearing the following Friday, June 2nd.

But that date would come, and go, due to the disappearance of a material witness. Margaret Dowdy departed Hutch twice for destinations unknown, foiling the attempts of sheriff's deputies to subpoena her. Her absence would cause three continuances before a preliminary hearing finally took place on June 29th.

* * * * *

Annas Brown chose a different brown dress, this one with a white collar, for her two-hour preliminary hearing on Thursday, June 29th. She did not take the witness stand but watched intently as five individuals took turns testifying. Only the appearance of Mrs. Lewis, the victim's mother, made the murderess divert her gaze. Perhaps she was influenced by the fact that Joy Malee Joy's young daughter, Vicki, had come to the hearing with her grandmother.

The physicians who had autopsied Joy Malee Joy reiterated their findings, including divergent opinions about the cause of death. Dr. G.A. Chickering noted that the victim, already weakened from the incomplete abortion, strangled on her throat mucus. Dr. L.C. Murphy restated his belief that excessive loss of blood had killed her, and referred to clear evidence of instrumentation.

Then Margaret Dowdy, whose absences had postponed the preliminary hearing, appeared. She claimed to have been unaware a hearing was scheduled, and had been visiting relatives in Dodge City. At the request of County Attorney Fontron, she was placed under $1,000 bond as a material witness.

Nurse Dowdy answered questions about the abortion after care, which she had been providing Annas Brown for a year and a half. She offered new descriptions of the dying girl, saying the abortionist had told Nurse Dowdy by phone that "the little girl from Pratt is pretty sick" and "is acting queer and turning blue." The nurse admitted that she had seen instruments (for abortion) in the Brown basement on previous visits but did not know what they were used for. She had seen no such instruments on the murder night, the nurse claimed.

Final testimony at the hearing came from funeral director Phil Johnson, Deputy Sheriff Gene Schroder, and the victim's mother.

Following the hearing's conclusion, Annas Whitlow Brown was ordered bound over to district court for trial. Its date was to be set when the September docket was determined.

CHAPTER THREE

THE INVINCIBLE MRS. BROWN
November, 1950

"Ye Gods!" The newspaper crackled in my father's hands as he crunched a corner and held it closer. "Snooky?" He called from the parlor toward the kitchen to ask whether she had read about the Brown case and that Hutch woman who murdered a young woman in an abortion. Three lawyers would represent her, he said. The trial was set to begin right before Thanksgiving.

She did not answer. So he began to tell me what the newspaper was reporting about this woman named Annas Brown. They depicted her as "portly" and "stout," he said with a snicker before reading more out loud. Then he began carrying on about the attorneys who were representing her. Their names were familiar from Bar Association meetings, he said, never indicating whether he actually knew them.

"What's an abortion?" I asked.

"Mrs. Tusswagon, you're a little too young to be hearing about that."

* * * * *

I could think of only one person who might be able to tell me about abortion and not rush out to gossip about my inquiry. Gracie was the wisest fifth grader I knew. Maybe it was because she lived in a trailer park that a tornado had swept through not long before. Afterward, my father had driven me past. Bits of technicolored clothing and sateen curtains dangled from tree limbs. A car was turned upside down with some kid's bike lying on top. Trailer parks seemed a magnet for twisters, if Mac was any indication.

42

Gracie was tough, my friends said. She wore sweaters with holes darned together, and shoes some sister had walked around in before her. She knew about things the rest of us did not. I had decided that was true after our girls-only health class lecture about menstruation. It had turned everyone's face red except hers. Gracie appeared unfazed and even had the nerve to ask the teacher a question. I thought maybe one of her big sisters had already told her all about it. The only sister of hers I had seen wore thick red lipstick and green eye shadow.

I waited for Gracie one day after gym class to ask my pre-rehearsed question. She treated it as if everyone but me knew what abortion was. "Killing babies," she said casually, as if choosing a flavor of ice cream. "It's illegal." She walked away.

* * * * *

At the time of this unheralded introduction of Annas Brown into our lives, my father never discussed whether he disapproved of her baby killing. I just assumed that to be fact. The ridicule he passed along to me about her hard-edged looks and tangible toughness led me to believe that her profession dismayed him. The thought of killing babies, unborn or otherwise, horrified me. All I could imagine was tiny helpless bodies whose lives were snuffed out as quickly as a candle flame. It never occurred to me to ask if it troubled him as much as it did me.

The only newborn baby I had ever seen him around was Andrea. They had brought her squalling bundle home from the Mac hospital on a suffocating July day. My mother had carried her into our parlor and sat with her in a velour chair. I had thought something was terribly wrong with my new sister, who would not stop screaming.

My father had kept circling the chair, seemingly more agitated by the moment. "For God's Sake," he had finally said. "What's wrong with her?"

"Nothing. She's a baby." My mother had shot a despairing look his way with eyes ringed from fatigue.

43

"Well, I have work to do at the office," he had said, swooping over her head to kiss her hair. "Try to get some sleep, Snooky."

* * * * *

Considering my father's passion for newspapers, I was not surprised when he pored daily over details of the sensational upcoming abortion trial. Mrs. Brown, as newspapers sometimes referred to her, seemed to intrigue him. Her unsavory activities reeked of murder, scandal and illegal derring-do. They were the sort of risque behaviors that he claimed made life "inn-trah-stiing."

For some reason, all seamy stories enchanted him. So did gossipy tales about the mischief-makers of Mac, who caused locals to seek details by asking one another, "Know any good dirt?" He liked to embellish their antics for us after Saturday nights out with them at the country club or at the Warren Hotel where the near-impossible feat of sinning privately in Mac transpired upstairs.

His favorite stories concerned lusty, busty and outrageous women. Veronica Paulson, Va-Va-VOOM as he called her, qualified for all three descriptions. Va-Va-VOOM was at it again, he told us some Sunday mornings. That dull oil man husband of hers could hardly handle his sassy blonde wife, he said. She would be better off back home in Texas.

Delores Swain, or DUM-de-dum-dum by his description, represented a Mac scandal that he could not seem to get enough of. She was pretty and had a husband so stupid that he failed to notice her affair with the salesman who visited their yard goods store almost daily. DUM-DE-DUM-DUM, he mocked, making swishy steps across the carpet with his nose in the air.

My mother must have enjoyed his renditions of these mini-scandals because they made her laugh, an unusual event that only prodded his exaggerations. "You would flirt with anything in a skirt," she kidded him, waiting for a denial that never came.

44

My father loved murder mysteries, too, almost as much as women. He seemed in awe of characters who crossed over an invisible line of morality to commit evil and then waited to see whether they would be found out. He talked about some of them to me, as if he were an actor and had stepped momentarily into their skins.

As he often reminded us, he had dazzled high school audiences with his thespian skills. He mesmerized them as Roger Shields ("A Young Chicago Blood") in The Whole Town's Talking and Pickney Herring ("The Town's Leading Citizen") in Smile, Rodney, Smile. He liked to show me a Student Council "Stunt Night" program, on which he had penned his own autograph: "Personal Appearance of Paul A. Lackie, World-Famed Actor and Speaker." Already a gadfly, he had also served on the Dramatic Club's Social Committee.

He bragged of his expertise as a newsman, too. This was based on his high-school tenure as a "Sports Spotter" for the McPherson Pied Life newspaper. "Lefty Lackie" had been his byline. It seemed odd since, other than toying briefly with tennis, he had never engaged in a sport.

Classmates had targeted his lofty political aspirations, even back then. Their high school newspaper "Hi-Lifers" column had noted:

"President Roosevelt has sent for Master Paul Lackie
to advise him on the present economic situation."

Those twin passions of politics and writing, punctuated by his obsession for affluence and ostentation, had flourished in a lengthy journalism assignment he titled "WEDDINGS." He fantasized about meeting his bride, "the comely and talented Miss Iva Beeinmibonnet" at Yale University. Her father was prominent Congressman Harper Brigham Beeinmibonnet, who boasted homes in Pudget Sound and New York City. At their "high noon" nuptials on July Fourth in New York City:

"The bride was attired in white velvet, trimmed in
pearls. Her going-away ensemble was of blue serge with
slippers, gloves, and hat to match. After a month's trip

to Europe, Mr. and Mrs. Lackie will make their home
at the Hotel Governor Clinton in New York City, where
Mr. Lackie divides his interests between his sports writing work with the Times and his weekly sport broad-
casts over the N.B.C."

Even in high school, he had fled his childhood home of shoo-away
demons to spin an imaginary life populated by glamorous luminaries
with him starring in the spotlight.

He had dabbled in poetry, submitting a piece to The Denver Post
Sunday magazine. He had also scribbled nonsensical rhymes like one
about his mother:

> "My name is Hattie
> Not so lean and not so fatty
> I like pretty dishes
> About them I am batty."

After high school, he had transported his thespian aspirations to
McPherson College, a Church of the Brethren facility just nine blocks
from home. His apparent penchant for romance not only landed him
the part of "Lucentio, suitor to Bianca" in The Taming Of The Shrew
but caused co-director Della Lehman to autograph his play program:
"Wishing you continued success in the gentle art of love."

His romantic inclinations were also noted in a lengthy item of the
"Spec-Yu-La-Shuns" column of McPherson College's The Spectator
newspaper:

> " ... Romeo, more commonly known as Paul
> Lackie, is back in our midst ... And can that boy work
> fast! ... Romeo would be seen chinning with one of
> the (girls) one day and with the other the next ... Now
> Romeo has gone for another dame ... We all wonder
> who will be next."

46

No doubt he must have added flash and dash on a campus of sober students who entered a campus arch inscribed: "Wisdom Expels Folly as Light Expels Darkness." The school newspaper had singled him out as a "tall" and "well dressed" history major who would be remembered for "his clever skits and his ready wit." Never having attended Sunday School though, he probably failed to set foot in the college's brick campus church embellished with white Gothic finials.

* * * * *

Some years later, my father was starring in newspapers in a different vein. By the time Annas Brown was grabbing headlines, his political appearances had become a constant presence on newspaper front pages, too. If we failed to read his printed views there, additional opportunities existed to hear them in our kitchen. His political rhetoric flew at my sisters and me as we sat at the counter, breakfasting on oatmeal and cinnamon toast. He leaned against the refrigerator as Pall Mall smoke tarnished the fragrance of his body pampered during "my toilette."

Each morning preceding these political soliloquies, he commandeered one of our two bathrooms all for himself. He spent chunks of time locked away there. His voice rose and fell as water ran and he warbled, "Take a quick shower and smell like a flower." He razor-cleaned his face, shaved and deodorized armpits, fussed with his receding hairline, donned a V-neck undershirt beneath the first of two daily dress shirts, drenched himself in thick cologne, and patted cheeks to stimulate color.

No matter how hard he massaged his cheeks, they could never match the rouge-swirled ones in countless formal portraits Hattie had someone photograph of him as a boy. As a child, his reddened cheeks had glowed above a fancy sailor suit with a bib collar. Later, they had appeared crimson below felt fedoras and natty suits with pocket scarves. He had flirted with the camera as if certain of future fame.

47

"You primp more than any woman," my mother said to him nearly every morning.

Acting as if he did not hear her, he talked to our bent heads and advised us of his upcoming day. He was lunching with that political hotshot who had so much clout. His presence was required that night at a fancy cocktail reception where so-and-so, the political bigwig he had already told us about, was appearing. He paused now and then to clear his throat, as if to place italics beneath his pieces of news. His glossy wing-tipped shoes shone below perfectly tailored pants legs. A "time to leave for school" declaration from my mother, who had failed to acknowledge his shining day, was the only means of curbing his one-way conversation.

"Dad always had to let us know what he was doing every day, what politicians he was with, and how important he was," Margo would remember later. "Every day was his most exciting ever. He couldn't deal with an ordinary one."

That my father was becoming legitimately famous as a politician was no surprise to me. I already thought he was, from what he told us every morning. He celebrated the presence of his photo on newspaper front pages by clipping stacks of articles that quoted him, and waved them before us. Once in awhile he handed a paper to me and said, "Notice that familiar face right there out front? Why don't you read about me, Mrs. Tusswagon?"

The Wichita Beacon featured him, and five other prominent Kansans, below a headline that said:

"THE BEACON TAKES OFF ITS HAT TO
THESE WORTHWHILE LEADERS"

A Chase County Leader boxed advertisement heralded his upcoming appearance in Cottonwood Falls at the Masonic Temple:

> "Old Fashioned Republican Rally. The Hon. Paul
> Lackie, McPherson State Chairman Young Republican,
> Will be the Chief Speaker."

"Where is Cottonwood Falls?" I asked, trying to show the interest he sought.

"Cotton, cotton ... that's a hot 'un," he began, testing rhymes to form a ditty. "Cotton, cotton ... " He never answered my question.

Sometimes newspapers even quoted the kind of diatribes we listened to as part of his general conversation. The Independence Daily Reporter was one:

> "I submit to you that the people do not want the
> 'hare-brained' schemes of Harry Truman and the pain-
> killers dealt from the carpet-bag of the Misery from
> Missouri ... "

His favorite part of the newspaper was the editorial page. Its content could set him off just as much as Va-Va-VOOM. He might screech something at us like, "What can those nincompoops writing for the Kansas City Star be thinking?" while reaching for scissors to clip it.

Political antics, especially by Democrats, riled him, too. Give-Em-Hell-Harry, the current president who hailed from across the state line in Missouri, got lambasted after my father spotted a headline in The Hutchinson News-Herald. It said:

"TRUMAN THREATENS TO BEAT UP MUSIC
CRITIC"

"Damn fool from Mizzou," he exploded. Just because some music expert had described the singing voice of presidential daughter Margaret as "flat" gave him no right to act like that, he said. "Typical damned dimwit Democrat."

Listening to him rant, I wondered occasionally what it would be like to have a dad who sat in his wing back chair calmly, read the newspaper silently, and did not engage in political diatribes. My best friend, Becky Carson, had a father like that. He came home every night after closing his store, sat and read with a tumbler of Scotch, complimented Mrs. Carson on her cuisine, and did not spout political theories at the dinner table. He moved through the rooms of their house like a steadying force rather than a speeding cyclone, did not rush off to Republican events after dinner, or fail even to show up as my father was doing more and more. He did not seem to covet coups like becoming governor, getting rich, or seeing his face in the newspaper either. All I could decide was that maybe Becky's father was not tuned to a life that was "inn-trah-stiing" like mine was. Though I grew weary of his words, the daily portraits of his exciting agendas made me long to skip school and follow him on certain adventures. Descriptions of his activities could transport me to arenas of possibility that no school project could, and replace my limited world of performing at chalkboards and reciting rhymes.

* * * * *

One Saturday afternoon, he bestowed an honor on me that prompted shivers of anticipation. He had finally acquiesced to my pleas to accompany him to one of his political speeches. Miraculously, my mother had agreed.

The name of the town whose citizens would rally to hear him has escaped my memory. We drove about two hours to reach this place. I did not attempt much conversation en route, leaving him alone to practice his upcoming remarks. Again and again, he ignited a Pall Mall after the cigarette lighter popped out of the dash.

After awhile, it began to rain. "We don't have an umbrella," I said.

"Mama and her umbrella, that's what we need," he said, offering one of his fake laughs. "Walked me to grade school under one, rain or shine, to and fro, ya know."

I struggled to imagine the awkwardly shaped boy I had seen in photographs, with his head too big for his scrawny body and knobby knees, huddled under an umbrella held by his scarecrow of a mother who was terrified about what lurked outdoors. They would traverse the steep steps outside her kitchen, creep across the concrete driveway and turn right, pass two old frame houses, cross the railroad tracks, and arrive at a school yard full of frolicking little kids.

"Even when the sun was out?" I glanced over and saw that his smile had gone away.

He ignited another cigarette. "Mama couldn't help it. She was worried something might happen to me." He shifted the cigarette to his left hand that gripped the steering wheel and reached his right one over to tap my knee. "You're my pretty best girl, eh Mrs. Tusswagon?" He waited before cranking up a country western tune on the radio to throb with laments about thwarted love.

"Yes."

"I love you. Do you love me, too?" He glanced my way.

"Yes."

He turned up the radio.

They had reserved a special parking spot for him, and we entered the backdoor of the hall. Local Republicans had festooned it with GOP banners and their symbolic elephants. Red, white and blue crepe paper hung in every corner. The man who greeted us seemed startled to see me standing there, clutching the hand of their speaker. He stammered that they had not arranged a seat for me on the platform, but surely could.

"I don't want to sit up there in front of all those strangers," I told my father. "Let me stay down in the audience."

"No. You belong up there with me, Mrs. Tusswagon."

So there I sat, feet dangling just above the surface of the floor. He introduced me to the crowd. "Folks, I want you to meet Cynthia. I call her Mrs. Tusswagon." I cringed as he continued. "She's the oldest of my three daughters. The Harem, I call them." He chuckled, then

51

waited for them to do the same. As if cued to be a game show audience that produced canned laughter, they responded. He turned to me and winked. My cheeks felt like a furnace had just kicked in behind them as my eyes locked onto the battered wood of the stage. I knew that I should stand up, as my mother had taught me. But I entertained visions of falling while trying to make my feet connect with the floor. It prompted me to lift one hand and make a little wave to a sea of faces. The gesture at once made me feel stupid and shy.

Adrenalin soared into the hall when he began speaking. The voice we had listened to on the radio, and in the bathroom, was connected to a real body now. It gyrated like a yo-yo behind the podium. The fine fabric of his pants legs vibrated with the energy emanating beneath them. His upper body joined the motion. Shoulders dipped. Hands trembled. He might have been palsied or composed of nerve endings, so great was his intent to motivate the crowd. He seemed born to speak, as instinctively as a baby swam in amniotic fluid. He was without fear, or a trembling voice. The words that streamed out were so much a part of him that he used no notes, and did not falter.

I would never come to understand what had produced this man who craved the rush that only a political crowd, which he mesmerized, could deliver. He might have been a drug addict, dependent on groups of strangers for his fix. It seemed impossible to me that a father like Perry, with an eighth-grade education, and a mother like Hattie, whose interest in reading was limited to quilt patterns, could have produced a son so swift and sure. But then I had never sat on Hattie's lap in her rocking chair, as he had, and listened to fantastic stories of jeweled princesses and flawless princes like a boy named Paul Andrew. I had not had to invent my own playmates because my mother would not allow real ones in our house, and dream up my own little melodramas in which I had to play all of the parts. And my mother, cranky though she was, had never kept me hostage in her kitchen or walked me to school beneath an umbrella.

After my father's speech, people with bright eyes and outstretched hands approached him. He towered over them and leaned his head down like a giraffe reaching for low tree leaves. He turned around now and then to look at me, still in my chair on the stage. His eyes brimmed with joy.

"How about that, Mrs. Tusswagon?" he said on the way home. "Went pretty well if I do say so myself. What'd ya think?"

"I ... "

"Get a load of that applause, eh?"

"Yes ... "

"That's ole P.A.L., wowing 'em." He reached over and tweaked my cheek, then lighted a cigarette.

* * * * *

As my father and Kansans all over the state were reading in newspapers about Annas Brown, she was preparing to face a jury who would decide her future.

THE STATE OF KANSAS vs. ANNAS WHITLOW BROWN was to be heard in the 1930 Hutchinson courthouse at 206 West First Street. The trial was recorded in official records as CASE NO. 38,342.

The defendant was hardly a novice at performing abortions. Yet she had no professional training. A specific count of babies destroyed by her hands was uncertain. She was a mother herself, with grown daughters named Lucille Updegraffe and Juanita Whitlow. Her legal name had been Mrs. John S. Brown before a divorce. Still, newspapers reporting on the case liked to call her Mrs. Brown. Apparently she and her ex-husband had remained amicable since he attended her trial and volunteered to play a significant role in her future.

There was jarring incongruity between the soft beauty of the Reno County district courtroom, where the trial was to take place, and the brutal ugliness of her crime. The second-floor chambers were a medley of arched ceiling panels of pale yellow, art deco sconces, and a striking wall mural behind the judge's chair. Burled wood railings divided the judge, jury and onlookers. It hardly seemed the appropriate setting for discussions of gushing blood, murdered babies, desperate women, or illegal butchering.

Nevertheless, the tumultuous trial was slated to begin here on the morning of Thursday, November 16th. Elsewhere in the world, crises were also occurring in locales that were far-flung from the Hutch courtroom. In North Korea, the number of American war casualties was nearing 29,000. Troops were battling in snowy conditions near the Manchurian border. Newspapers were printing solemn observations about the loss of lives.

In central Kansas, the murder trial that focused on the loss of one complete life and another not yet launched began its one-week run as a media event. The first obstacle proved to be jury selection. In the six months since the murder, this sensational case had assumed a hurdy-gurdy quality. Everyone seemed to know about it and had formed strong opinions.

No one had been convicted in Reno County for performing an abortion in 40 years, according to The Hutchinson News-Herald. Back in 1910, abortionist Emeline Hatch had been found guilty of second-degree manslaughter. But various attempts since then to convict other abortionists had failed.

Judge F. B. Hettinger was to preside over the Brown case. Coincidentally, his uncle James Hettinger had been the county attorney during that 1910 trial.

Day One of the proceedings was consumed by jury selection. Thirty-five potential jurors had been chosen for the original pool. However, most were rejected because of preconceived opinions. Day One passed, and the jury was still incomplete.

* * * * *

As Day Two began on Friday, November 17th, a suitable stable of jurors remained to be chosen. Overseas, war continued to rage in Korea. In England, opposition leader Winston Churchill reminded the House of Commons to "thank God" that British war casualties numbered just one to every 200 for America.

In Hutch, jury selection was finally completed by afternoon. Not a single woman was among those chosen. Each individual who would decide Annas Brown's fate was male.

Throngs of curious people showed up to vie for seats in the small courtroom. A preponderance of women, "most with gray hair," were on hand, according to Hutch newspaper reporter James Skinner. A local minister attended the first day and every one thereafter. Even attorneys who were not involved in the case arrived to take seats.

This assortment of humanity became so engrossed as spectators that they interfered with the proceedings. Even attorneys could not contain their passion about the case. One of them blurted, "He shouldn't have done that," when he disagreed with another lawyer's question. A woman in the audience, who must have imagined that she possessed inside information about the crime, volunteered to answer a question that an attorney asked of a witness. Giggling from spectators contributed to the overall bedlam, too. That prompted the judge to reprimand them and threaten to evict anyone else who laughed out loud.

All of this chaos prompted a court official to enforce a "no standing room allowed" dictum. Bailiff Mike Fitzgerald, who positioned himself in a doorway to block unauthorized entrances, cracked, "Call 'em for jury duty, and they'd say they didn't have time to serve."

The local press did its part to fan the furor. The Hutchinson News-Herald ran a headline proclaiming:

"SELDOM A DULL MOMENT FOR CROWDS
WHICH GATHERED AT UNIQUE TRIAL"

An editorial in the same newspaper referred to a "crowd-drawing abortion case" which:

> " ... had its hour of glory when it drew housewives away from 'John's Other Wife' (soap opera) and turned strong men's thoughts from the threatening excess profits tax."

Even the emotional daughters of the accused added to the daily circus atmosphere. Lucille Updegraffe and Juanita Whitlow broke into tears frequently and jumped up to rush out of the courtroom.

The heartbreaking daily presence of Joy Malee Joy's six-year-old daughter underscored the tragedy of this crime. She arrived each day with the victim's mother, Mrs. Lewis. The child sat in a seat reserved for her up front beside her grandmother. During the proceedings, she cradled and rocked the doll she had brought, or positioned it on her lap. When her mother's name was spoken, she glanced up briefly at her grandmother. Then she returned to tending her doll.

For the trial, the Browns had hired a trio of attorneys to keep their abortionist out of prison. Two of them, Don Shaffer and Abraham Weinlood, were from Hutchinson. The third, A.D. Weiskirch, was from Wichita.

Leading the prosecution team were Assistant County Attorney John R. Alden of Hutchinson, and Harold R. Fetzer, State Attorney General. Assisting them was outgoing Reno County Attorney John Fontron. This was his final case for the county, and he would later serve on the Kansas Supreme Court. Backing him was Assistant County Attorney Fred C. Preble.

At the outset, Attorney Preble advised jurors about the business card listing Annas Brown and Margaret Dowdy that had been found in the victim's purse.

Then he summoned R. T. Davis, the snoopy Hutch service station attendant, to the witness stand to describe his interaction with Joy Malee Joy. Davis, who probably never dreamed he would have the rapt attention of an entire courtroom, related how she had strolled into his station and asked to use the telephone. He admitted listening in on a conversation in which she asked someone's permission to arrive somewhere for an appointment. Afterward, he had watched her drive across the street, park, and enter a house. He did not say whether he knew Annas Brown personally or the nature of her profession.

Others who stepped forward to recount their knowledge of the victim's demise included Phil Johnson, the funeral director and ambulance driver who had discovered the bloody body in the basement and transported it to the hospital.

Then Dr. C. W. Haines testified that Joy Malee Joy had been dead upon arrival at the hospital at 7:35 p.m.

The victim's employer also took a turn on the stand. Kins Monger, owner of the Pratt firm where she had worked, recreated the beginning of the murderous night. His employee had left the office about five o'clock, he said. She had used a prior appointment as her excuse not to attend an office party that evening.

Finally, the pair of police officers who had visited the Brown residence about 9 p.m. following the murder related their encounter with the abortionist. Detective John Robinson and Deputy Sheriff Gene Schroder recalled how she claimed not to have known the victim until meeting her outdoors on the sidewalk and volunteering use of her home's bathroom when the "little girl" indicated a need for one. When this total stranger had become ill inside her house, she put her on an upstairs bed. Later, she had retracted that version of the story and admitted taking her to the basement instead.

* * * * *

The following morning, Friday November 17th, County Attorney John Fontron opened the scandalous trial by grilling Margaret Dowdy, the nurse who worked in collaboration with the abortionist.

Nurse Dowdy proved to be as slippery in her testimony as Annas Brown had been with the detectives who visited her home on the night Joy Malee Joy died. The issue around which she danced with County Attorney Fontron was "bed rest."

"For what malady or condition did you care for the patients?" he asked.

"Bed rest."

"Bed rest for what condition? Why did the patient need bed rest?"

"I don't know just exactly how to state that."

"What was wrong with the patients?" County Attorney Fontron persisted.

"I can't say exactly," Nurse Dowdy dodged.

"Tell the jury what the condition of the patient was and why the patient needed bed rest."

"You don't have to have a reason for bed rest."

At that point, the judge lost his patience. "Answer the question. Tell what the bed rest was for," he ordered Nurse Dowdy.

The county attorney had become so frustrated that he declared her a "hostile witness" and recounted her similarly sketchy answers during a preliminary hearing in the case. He read that testimony as evidence:

"What did the patients need bed rest for?" County Attorney Fontron had asked the nurse.

"They were sent for after care."

"After care for what?"

"After care for an abortion."

Finishing that prior testimony, he turned to the nurse and asked, "Is that statement true?"

"Yes."

"Did Mrs. Brown ever send patients to you for another cause?"

"Not that I recall."

When asked if she knew what techniques the abortionist used to perform her work, the nurse said, "No."

The county attorney then zeroed in on the specifics of Joy Malee Joy's connection to the abortionist and herself. The nurse admitted that she had spoken twice on the telephone with Annas Brown about the "little girl" from Pratt.

Two weeks before the scheduled abortion, Mrs. Brown had told her the girl was five months pregnant and would be coming to the nurse's home for after care following the "treatment." Then she had telephoned a second time to advise that the girl's "treatment" was being postponed and would probably occur a week later.

The night of the murder, according to Nurse Dowdy, she had received two phone calls from the abortionist. First, Annas Brown had called from her basement to say that "the little girl from Pratt" was at her house but might not be coming to the Dowdy residence, as planned, for after care.

The next call, thirty minutes later, had been much more urgent. Something had gone wrong. Nurse Dowdy said Annas Brown told her, "The girl had turned blue following the treatment, and something should be done about it."

Like her abortionist colleague, Nurse Dowdy had a shady professional reputation. That was revealed when defense attorney Don Shaffer cross-examined her. His questions forced her to admit that she had previous experience with abortions before hooking up with Mrs. Brown. She had formerly worked for a Lewis, Kansas, physician who was arrested for performing abortions.

In order to prove their respective cases, the defense and prosecution attorneys presented differing theories about what might have caused the pregnant woman's death.

Dr. L.C. Murphy, a pathologist who had conducted an autopsy on Joy Malee Joy, testified next. His conclusion was: "Loss of blood following an abortion caused the death of Mrs. Joy." He added that it was "possible but not probable" that the abortion could have been performed at a different location than the one where Mrs. Joy was picked up by an ambulance. He had found no evidence of poison, which could have caused an abortion, in the victim's stomach, said Dr. Murphy. "In my opinion, it was a criminal abortion."

The doctor, at the request of a defense attorney, stepped to a blackboard and diagrammed a woman's abdomen in order to demonstrate how an abortion was performed and the mistake made in the case of Joy Malee Joy.

Dr. G. A. Chickering, the coroner who had performed the autopsy with Dr. Murphy, disagreed with his colleague about the cause of death. Asphyxiation was the reason, he said. Due to initial shock and bleeding, the victim could not clear mucus from her windpipe, he theorized.

With those factors established for consideration, court was recessed for the weekend.

* * * * *

On Monday, November 20th, testimony in the Brown trial was set to resume at nine o'clock in the morning.

By now, daily accounts of the abortion revelations were vying with the Korean War for the primary news spot on front pages of The Hutchinson News-Herald. Articles referring to "manslaughter" and "bloody underwear" ran side by side with those detailing "the new menace" of China and "Red resistance."

In the Hutch courtroom, the state used the trial's first hour to conclude its case. One of their final witnesses was William C. Woolston. He was a chemist at the laboratory of the State Board of Health who had examined the contents of the victim's stomach following her autopsy. "Did you find any traces of poison?" County Attorney Fontron asked.

"I found none."

Then it was the Brown defense team's turn to roll out its ammunition. But first, Attorney Weinlood attempted to have his client's case dismissed. He told Judge Hettinger that the state had failed to produce sufficient evidence to support the charges against her. He also contended that the case had been improper because the abortionist should have been charged under a different statute.

The judge barely considered the request before overruling the motion.

So defense Attorney Weiskirch addressed the jury: "We will show that she (Mrs. Joy) did not die of an attempted abortion; that she did not bleed to death; that death resulted from a collection of mucus in her trachea."

He called a Wichita chest physician, Arthur L. Ashmore, as the first defense witness.

"What, in your opinion, caused the death of Joy Malee Joy?" the attorney asked the doctor, whose knowledge of the case stemmed from reading the autopsy report.

"Asphyxiation. Smothering, in other words."

In response to a prior question, the physician said, "It is my opinion that she did not bleed to death." Her asphyxiation, he added, "could have been caused by gasping for breath while vomiting or by drugs which affect the respiratory center of the brain."

The most graphic description of how Joy Malee Joy died would be issued later and documented in the court syllabus. The report would state that "the tearing of the placenta was by a metal instrument which managed to pass the water bag without puncturing it, that the result of this separation would have been an enormous gush of blood, which would be exceedingly difficult to control, that there would have been sufficient loss of blood to lead to a condition of shock." It would also observe: "Her placenta showed evidence of instrumentation with the tear being ragged and with bits of tissue hanging."

The defense concluded its presentation in time for court to recess for the night.

* * * * *

On Tuesday morning, two days before Thanksgiving, it was time to convene once again in the Hutch courtroom.

If the mood was chaotic here, it was much more so in Nevada and California where killer floods were rampaging. Nine people had died. Las Vegas casinos and hotels were inundated with six to eight feet of water. And in nearby New Mexico, 100 prison convicts were rioting behind walls of the state penitentiary. Yet the nation's annual holiday was imminent, causing President Truman to issue "A Proclamation" in honor of Thanksgiving Day.

Tuesday's courtroom atmosphere was as grim as the Western floods and prison riot.

Assistant County Attorney Preble made one last stab at sending Annas Brown to prison. He ticked off the timetable of the victim making an abortion appointment, walking into the Brown residence, and being carried out to an ambulance shortly afterward.

Then, as if to emphasize the grizzly aspects of the case one last time, he made a memorable gesture. He held up before jurors the blue jeans and blouse that the victim had been wearing the night she and her fetus lost their lives. Look at these clothes, he said. They were not bloody. One might think that a crime had never been committed. But what was beneath those garments was a different story. The victim had been carried out of the Brown house and died in underwear drenched with blood. That changed the picture entirely. It proved that someone had put her unsoiled clothes on over the blood-soaked underpants after the botched abortion, he said.

Those jurors who glanced over at Annas Brown to assess her reaction encountered an extraordinary sight. As Attorney Preble stood before them describing the blood and mutilation she had created, the abortionist paid no attention. She was preoccupied with filing her fingernails, as if she were at home in the privacy of her bathroom.

Assistant County Attorney Alden pitched guilt to the jurors, too, saying that the victim's wounds "could have been produced only by an instrument of abortion inserted to perform an abortion." Joy Malee Joy "died directly at the hands of Mrs. Brown," he concluded. "You have a duty to society to put this proved abortionist out of business." As he pointed his finger at Annas Brown, she ignored him.

The defense countered by attempting to paint Mrs. Brown as a female Good Samaritan and by attaching blame to the victim.

"It is unfortunate that Mrs. Joy placed herself in a situation in which she needed help," said Attorney Shaffer. "Mrs. Brown is being tried for attempting to help an unfortunate out of her troubles."

He urged the jury to use their knowledge of mankind while reaching a verdict and attempted to deflect responsibility away from her. The only evidence that Mrs. Brown was an abortionist stemmed from another abortionist, he said. "Mrs. Dowdy admitted to you on the witness stand that she had been in the abortion business for years."

Following that, legal summations were concluded. It was time for the jury to deliberate. Before issuing instructions to them, Judge Hettinger made a comment about the accused. That Annas Brown did not testify in her own defense should not be held against her, he suggested.

Then he outlined criteria on which to base the abortionist's extent of guilt. Two basic questions must be answered by the jury to determine the severity of punishment.

First: What was the cause of death?

Second: Was the aborted fetus categorized as a "vitalized embryo," or a "quick child" who evidenced movement?

The second question seemed to confound everyone, including the jurors. Aborting a "quick child," according to Kansas statutes, could be punished only with second-degree manslaughter. Punishment was harsher for aborting a "vitalized embryo," which was not "quick." That qualified as first-degree manslaughter, assuming that abortion caused the death.

An editorial in The Hutchinson News-Herald excoriated the legislation that created these rules:

" ... The trial also showed clearly that Kansas criminal procedure is often hamstrung, confusing and downright ridiculous because state laws have been permitted to grow up like Topsy. Criminal statutes are conflicting, mysterious, and often meaningless...

Three separate statutes deal with abortion. All were passed by the legislature in 1868 ... The way the laws read, killing an unborn child old enough to kick is second degree; killing one younger is first degree. If there should be a difference, which there shouldn't, one would think it would be the other way. Obviously the state needs a single, clear abortion law ... "

About 1:30 in the afternoon, the jury prepared to leave and begin deliberating the fate of Annas Brown. Judge Hettinger advised that they could choose one of three sentences: guilty of performing an abortion, which would merit a jail sentence or fine, or both; not guilty; or guilty of first-degree manslaughter, with five to 21 years in prison.

Should they opt for the first degree, by far the harshest verdict, they must be satisfied that the victim was pregnant with a "vitalized embryo" and not a "quick child" at the time of abortion, that the defendant used abortion instruments on the victim, and that the abortion killed the victim.

Suspense hovered in the courtroom over homemakers who would normally be in their kitchens preparing holiday cranberry sauce and pumpkin pie, attorneys who were stealing time away from their work, and a minister who should probably have been busy writing his Thanksgiving sermon. The Hutchinson News-Herald intensified the decision-day melodrama with a prominent front-page headline:

"JOY DEATH CASE TO JURY TODAY"

It ran above one far more frivolous, which probably titillated the curious as surely as this sensational trial:

"ASKS DIVORCE AFTER HUSBAND MADE HER SAVE DISHWATER"

Elsewhere in the newspaper, Thanksgiving grocery bargains prevailed. Hostesses could shop for holiday fixings like: potatoes, twenty-nine cents for ten pounds; celery for turkey stuffing, eight cents per pound; and coffee to accompany pumpkin pie, seventy-six cents a pound.

Yet spectators in the packed Hutchinson courtroom were focused on justice, not on Thanksgiving cuisine. So everyone waited.

Around four o'clock, the jury sent the judge a message. They asked for clarification on the difference between charges of first-degree manslaughter and misdemeanor in performing an abortion.

At five minutes past four, just two and one-half hours after they had begun deliberations, jurors filed back into the courtroom. Annas Brown was present, as were her attorneys. Her daughters were not, though they rushed in following the verdict.

The usual court formalities proceeded, and Court Clerk Irma Williams was asked to read the verdict.

"Guilty of manslaughter in the first degree," she said.

The defendant might as well have heard that she had been found innocent. She maintained her passive composure, but lowered her head. The only clues that the prospect of prison might be daunting were that she ran her tongue across her lips, and the color on her face intensified. Surprisingly, no one else in court displayed emotion either despite their earlier outbursts.

One of her attorneys requested that the jurors be polled individually. That did cause Annas Brown to react. She looked up and watched as each affirmed his "guilty" vote.

Afterward, she was taken away to be fingerprinted at the sheriff's office before being released on a $7,500 bond. She was also ordered to have a new bond in the same amount by the next day at noon, or she would be jailed.

The Brown attorneys announced immediately that they intended to seek a new trial for their client. Judge Hettinger chose the Saturday after Thanksgiving as the date by which the retrial motion must be filed. He also instructed that its hearing must take place before December 20th.

As a result of the bid for a new trial, Annas Brown's sentencing was delayed pending the outcome.

There was no way to know how, or where, the murderess spent her Thanksgiving Day. It was probable that she met with her trio of attorneys. For while our family was feasting on roasted turkey, mashed potatoes and gravy, creamed onions, homemade cranberry sauce, Parker house rolls, mandarin orange Jell-O salad, broccoli baked with cheese, pumpkin and pecan pie, the Brown legal team was hustling. They had less than 48 hours to conjure justifications for a new trial.

* * * * *

The day after Thanksgiving, The Hutchinson News-Herald entertained holiday revelers with a front page photo of a food-laden table with the caption:

"IT WAS FUN WHILE IT LASTED, BUT
THERE ALWAYS COMES A DAY AFTER"

For the Brown attorneys, that day after was strictly serious as they appeared back in court before Judge Hettinger. According to them, their client was the only one not at fault for her guilty verdict. They tried to convince the judge that the jury had bumbled their responsibility and engaged in misconduct. This implied that the trial had been unfair. The jury also received evidence that had not been authorized by the court, they contended. So that had thwarted justice by misdirecting them in material matters of the law. There was also new evidence, they said, that the verdict was contrary to that which had been presented. The court issued erroneous rulings and instructions, too. And the verdict had been procured by corruption of the plaintiff, they suggested.

Perhaps the most abstract reason of the 17 justifications for a new trial they had created during Thanksgiving Day planning was that the verdict was given under the influence of passion and prejudice.

While the attorneys pleaded on behalf of their client, The Hutchinson News-Herald reminded taxpayers of the mounting costs of the courtroom spectacle. "Bills resulting from the investigation and the trial of Mrs. Brown are still pouring into the district court clerk's office," it noted. "The total now reaches about $3,600 (about $27,000 today). Still to be added are mileage expenses incurred by some jurymen."

* * * * *

As the attorneys were trotting out their theories in Hutch, The Harem, Mom, Hattie, and Perry at the wheel of his Packard were heading there. The lure was Pegues' annual post-Thanksgiving sale. As was tradition, Hattie had dictated that we must attend to snatch bargains.

It was never a question of the hour at which we had to depart Mac for the big Pegues sale. Hattie expected us to be at the front door, vying for space with a flood of other shoppers, when the doors were unlocked. She knew that her faithful salesclerks would be eagerly awaiting her arrival to showcase handbags, jewelry, gloves, dresses, suits, shoes and hats for her consideration and their sales commissions. "Singing for their supper," my father said, likening the clerks to chirping birds.

Once inside the store, my mother always raced away from us in search of her own finds. That left Perry to tend my sisters and me in a place devoid of activities for children.

As usual, my father did not accompany us on this commercial marathon. He bade us farewell with vague excuses about Saturday morning work to do at his office with his secretary, or urgent political duties that required his attention. "Mrs. Tusswagon, someone has to support The

Harem," he would say, jiggling my cheek while delivering us to the Marlin Street driveway.

"Paul Andrew, what can I bring you?" Hattie would entreat, extending a shaking gloved hand from her front car window.

"Oh Mama, remember that list I gave you last time?" he would answer before speeding off to destinations unknown.

As the Packard inched out of the driveway, we could count on the sight of him waiting there near dusk when we returned, eager to find out what Mama had brought him.

Had a seer been on hand that particular Friday to predict my father's future, he might have advised him to accompany us to Hutch. That wise wizard would probably have suggested that he spend his day there at the courthouse. He could have listened to Annas Brown's attorneys, desperate to keep their client out of prison, outline the reasons why she had not received a fair trial. He would have heard Judge Hettinger conclude, after considering the entire list, that he wanted this case settled before the calendar rolled from 1950 to 1951. He would also have gleaned tidbits about this crime that had never appeared in newsprint. He could even have seen the abortionist in person and gazed into his own future.

* * * * *

Several weeks later and two days short of their deadline, Annas Brown and her attorneys gathered in Hutch district court once again. It was the 18th of December, with one week remaining until Christmas. The focal point chosen by defense lawyers this time was the "quick child" issue.

Attorney Don Shaffer argued that the prosecution had not proven "beyond a reasonable doubt" that the dead embryo was not "quick." Considering that, he contended that his client deserved second-degree manslaughter charges instead of first.

The three-hour appeal proceedings were even more chaotic than those at the first trial. A focal point was the testimony of Lena Gilmore, who lived in Hutch. She was a friend of Mrs. Lewis, the mother of the victim.

Attorney Shaffer said that Mrs. Lewis had visited Lena Gilmore's house the day after her daughter died. The distraught mother confessed then that she had known her daughter was pregnant. Joy had felt the baby's movement, she said. And she blamed herself for having sent her cherished child to Annas Brown. "I feel like I'm to blame for sending Joy to Hutchinson to see some nurse," the victim's mother had supposedly said.

Lena Gilmore also testified that Mrs. Lewis had said, referring to Annas Brown: "When I get through with that old lady, I won't have any more worries, because she'll pay plenty."

Courtroom sparks began to fly after the revelation that Lena Gilmore had told Attorney Shaffer, prior to this court appearance, of reading that Mrs. Lewis testified she had been unaware that her daughter was pregnant. She claimed to have read it in The Hutchinson News-Herald.

That made County Attorney Fontron livid. He accused Lena Gilmore of lying about her conversation with Mrs. Lewis and threatened to file perjury charges against her.

Suspecting that her testimony was false, the county attorney sent sheriff's officers to impound copies of The Hutchinson News-Herald that had been printed daily during the trial. Once they arrived in the courtroom, he presented them to Lena Gilmore. He ordered her to point out exactly where she had read about Mrs. Lewis's testimony.

"I won't do it," she told him.

Then he asked her to read the datelines of the newspapers, all of which featured extensive trial coverage but did not mention testimony by Mrs. Lewis.

Again, she refused.

So County Attorney Fontron appealed to the court to force her to point out the item.

As the attorneys became combative over the issue, Judge Hettinger intervened. "No use going on with this," he said. "I'm not taking this business of new evidence very seriously anyway." He had decided not to grant the abortionist a new trial, he announced.

Annas Brown's sole response to the negative news was a flushed face.

Her attorneys refused to be dented by the verdict. They declared they would appeal the judge's decision to the Kansas Supreme Court.

Within days, they would do so. Their efforts would be unsuccessful.

Annas Brown was sentenced to begin her prison term of five to 21 years at the State Industrial Farm for Women in Lansing.

CHAPTER FOUR

OUR LET'S-PRETEND FAMILY
1951-53

Abe's birthday represented cause for double celebrations at our house. At least, my father believed so. As if predestined, Margo, or "Snussy Puss" as he called her, had been born on February 12th just like Abe.

Each year, while devouring her beloved chocolate birthday cake, Margo had to listen to him rhapsodize about Abe. He compared himself to his hero until their images melded into one. By then, we were accustomed to his regular pilgrimages to Springfield as if treading the Illinois streets his idol once had might transform him by osmosis. And all of us were very weary of hearing that Abe's family hailed from Macon County and Perry's from Macoupin County, as if the two Illinois families must have been related.

"Think of what we have in common!" he said, eyes glittering. "Abe said this ...," he might intone as if they had just finished a conversation.

Moments like that made me wonder if he fantasized about being destined to become as famous as Abe. His association with the martyred president seemed to transcend the normal adulation of such a hero. It was so profound that he might have been exchanging his own personality for that of Abe during soliloquies about him. His voice shifted. His head tilted a bit. He assumed a slightly bent posture. Sometimes he recited portions of his speeches from memory. Right there before us, he stepped out of his own persona and into one that he coveted. It mirrored his easy access to a world of delusions, where he could be anyone he wanted.

Margo watched him with eyes that were a paler blue version of his.

She must have wondered why her birthday was less important than a dead president named Abe. She got to have chocolate cake every year but never a celebration completely her own.

After her fifth birthday in 1950, Margo no doubt hoped that the Abe ballyhoo would never again reach the crescendo it had that year. Her birth date had been totally eclipsed by my father's invitation to appear as a political star at a Lincoln Day Rally in Independence, Kansas.

The hoopla had begun several weeks before with an invitation issued by The Lincoln Day Club, which featured a portrait of Abe wearing a bow tie. He propped it on our fireplace mantle and smiled fondly at it. His anticipation intensified daily as February 12th approached.

We had been subjected to incessant dress rehearsal deliveries of his Lincoln speech. Words had rolled off his tongue like dice circling a roulette wheel. He intended to wow a luncheon gathering at Independence's Kansas Hotel, he had informed us. He would employ strong language and daring proposals to do so, and would earn a follow-up Lincoln Day Club letter of commendation noting: "Everyone was very much impressed with your address."

His remarks would be printed afterward on the front page of the Kansas City Star, which would note "Lackie Speaks Boldly" and describe a "frank approach to G.O.P. woes:"

> "We'd better get a program a long way removed from the program we have now (as a party), if we're going to be successful. Young Republicans have an honest desire for candidates and issues salable to the American people. I believe the Republican party nationally would do well to pay attention to the so-called dissatisfied and discontented youth of Kansas."

The Independence Daily Reporter would allude to his strong remarks, too, before quoting his text:

72

"Lackie cast oratorical scorn at the present administration, which, in his opinion, is weak in its lack of policy and unsound programs. For some years the American people have been asking for positive issues and for positive actions …

This is but their rightful due and something which we, as Republicans, can furnish them, and which we as Republicans, intend to furnish them … "

But first came those dress rehearsals. As he had droned on with segments of his upcoming speech, Margo kicked me under the table.

"Ouch!"

He had ignored us and continued as my mother delivered a "That's enough" glare.

"There need be no question in our minds concerning the interest of young Americans in the politics and government of their nation. Our concern should be rather in arousing interest to the point of active participation in the politics which formulate that government. It can be aroused."

"What do ya think?" He had looked at me.

"Great, Dad." My mouth was half full of oatmeal.

"How many times have I told you not to speak until you've finished chewing?" Mom had chimed in.

"Snooky, don't be so hard on Mrs. Tusswagon. She's just trying to help."

"Mr. Pops, will you be here for my birthday party?" Margo had implored.

"Snussy Puss, I'll do my best. But you know Mr. Pops is pretty important now. You understand, don't you, that I must go where Abe calls me." He had laughed as she looked away.

Two years had gone by, and Margo's seventh birthday had safely passed, when the specter of Abe invaded our house again.

"Ye Gods, how about this!" My father, whose lack of physical coordination was often noted by my mother, was attempting to dance about the kitchen. In his hand was a cream-colored document that he finally held up for us to see. At the top, staring back, was a picture of Abe.

"Read it for them, Paul." Mom interrupted his off-key rendition of "Sheee-kah-go, Sheee-kah-go, that won-eeeer-full tawn."

> "You are hereby appointed Honorary Assistant Sergeant-at-Arms of the Republican National Convention. Please report at Convention Headquarters, Chicago, for duty at the Convention, not later than 10 A.M. July seventh."

He decided to travel by train to the Chicago convention. His leave-taking required our requisite farewell ritual, acted out this time on the platform at Perry's depot. All of us, except Hattie, surrounded him in the suffocating air. He delivered exuberant kisses, tweaked cheeks, and spread endearments while juggling a hang-up bag on one shoulder. It contained yet another new silk suit, compliments of Hattie. The pungent scent of his cologne floated about us, and it seemed the train would never arrive.

As we stood waiting, I listened to him ramble and thought that Chicago must be very far away and 500 times the size of Mac. He described a lake that extended as far as the eye could travel, skyscrapers you could see from miles away, and a major league baseball team with its very own stadium. "Sheee-kah-go" he warbled as shrieking whistles of the approaching train began to drown him out. My heart beat faster thinking about the exciting place where he was headed, like that rollicking "Around The World With Paul Andrew Lackie" school essay he had shown me once. I only wished that I could hop on board with him and join his latest adventure.

* * * * *

Several days later, we reassembled on the worn wood planks of the train platform. It was the heart of summer. Mac was still displaying its July Fourth flags at every light fixture along Main Street, though they barely moved in the thick sludge of air. My friends were off splashing in the cool waters of Mac's municipal pool. I had begged my mother that morning for a release from the ritual of greeting our returning politician so I could join them. But she insisted that his feelings would be hurt if everyone did not go. She did not seem to notice that our family had become obligated to perform a political mini-rally each time my father swept in and out of our lives. Or maybe she did recognize it but said nothing.

After all, she and the rest of us realized that folks in Mac considered him a genuine political celebrity by then. Should we forget, he had only to remind us that the McPherson newspaper had crowed about his Young GOP win:

> "May the community produce many more of such stature and prominence in public affairs."

They had featured him on the front page, too, when he departed for war:

> "Paul A. Lackie, local attorney, received his orders yesterday morning to report to the University of Arizona at Tucson, Arizona, August 16. He has an Ensign D-V (S) Commission ... Mr. Lackie has been a partner in the law firm of Cassler and Lackie for the last seven months. During his absence, Senator James A. Cassler will handle the practice ... Mrs. Lackie and daughter will remain in McPherson."

75

Now his proud Mac constituents could read about him in newspapers printed all about the Sunflower State. "Don't mind if I do say so myself, I've done Mac right proud," he liked to say.

Finally, we heard the roar of his train on its approach down the tracks. We had not brought homemade "Welcome Home" banners or small flags to hold. Instead, we waved our hands as he appeared in a train doorway. He filled its space. His head nearly grazed the top of the door frame, and his silk suit rippled like a sail in the train exhaust.

Once we were in the Cadillac, he could not seem to stop spilling the convention details. Red, white and blue balloons floating in clusters to the ceiling of the huge center. Bands blasting songs to salute the Grand Old Party and our glorious U.S. of A. Voices chanting and bodies swaying in celebration. Why, this event completely eclipsed that Boston political convention last year when he had served as delegate for the national gathering of Young Republicans, he raved.

It made me think of the letter he had sent us from there. It was filled with superlatives about listening to Connecticut Governor John Lodge speak at historic Plymouth Rock, visiting Old North Church, and rubbing shoulders with all kinds of famous politicians.

"I signed that letter with the quill Paul Revere used," he had boasted, searching our faces for reaction. "You know the story, 'Listen my children and you shall hear …'"

As the car crept now through Mac, it began to seem as if his lavish descriptions about Chicago would never cease, and we were to ride forever as his captive. Even so, his vivid word pictures managed to transport me to a city of skyscrapers and a cavernous building, where he stood waving a GOP banner and shouting "God bless America!"

Then finally, it ended. At least the cross-town auto trip did. Inside our house, he had one final flourish to add. He looked at each of us, pulled something purple and gold from his suit jacket pocket, and held it in an outstretched hand. It was two pieces of bronze separated by a purple ribbon. The top half was cast with an eagle and inscribed

76

"Honorary Assistant Sergeant-At-Arms." The part dangling below the ribbon featured a profile of Abraham Lincoln. His head was surrounded by "Chicago 1952" and "Republican National Convention."

My father ran his fingers across the memento that he was to save for the rest of his life and pinned it to his suit jacket lapel. "Abe and me," he murmured, his lips curling with satisfaction.

* * * * *

Maybe his dashing here and there, or his haphazard approach to everything, was the major contributor. Or perhaps it was politics. For some reason, there was an unspoken yet palpable sense in our house that my father was changing. He seemed to be turning into a hybrid of good and bad that was replacing what used to be mostly good. It felt so to me, at least.

He still swirled about us like a meteor, swooping down to pat our heads or tug at our cheeks before departing. He was heading for some political soiree, where cocktails would flow like swollen streams, or traveling to deliver a speech in some unknown burg. We had become used to that part of it.

It was the ominous absences when he simply failed to come home that were part of his new badness, and began to gnaw at me. On such nights, we sat at the dinner table and followed my mother's lead by ignoring his empty plate and melted ice in his glass. "Pass the cauliflower to the right, NOT the left," she said, dismissing Andrea's "Where's Dad?"

We would wait for him past the usual dinner time. My ears were tuned to hear the slam of his car door in the garage. My eyes were ready to examine his gait and assess the quantity of vodka consumed at the Legion, VFW, or somewhere else. But he did not come. So we pretended that an invisible guest, who ate and drank nothing, was occupying his chair.

Sometime later, in the black of night, I would awaken to the sound of voices down the upstairs hall. "You can't hold your liquor," my mother railed. He slurred to defend himself as she continued the volley. "Why do you care more about politics than us, and hang around with people like them?"

Once in awhile, his absences turned into crises. One late night, a ringing telephone summoned me to my parents' bedroom. Since my mother resolutely refused to answer such calls, the duty had become mine.

"Hello."

A nurse at the McPherson hospital was phoning to say that my father had been in a car accident. He was okay and very lucky, she said. Glass splinters in his forehead and neck, which would work their way out eventually, were his only injuries. I heard him talking as a backdrop to the medical report. Then she handed over the phone.

"Hi darlin'," he said in his thick vodka voice. "Had a lil' encounter with a light pole. Guess I'm like that cat with nine lives. Is your mother there?"

I turned to shake her shoulder and said there had been an accident. She rolled over and groaned.

"Mom will talk to you tomorrow," I told him.

"I love you, Mrs. Tusswagon. Do you love me, too?" I heard the plea that lurked in his voice.

Perhaps it was that night, or another one like it, when I appointed myself as Night Watchman of our house. I lay in bed awake, or read with a flashlight under my covers, and listened for the crunch of his car tires. Sleep would not come until he was safely home. No one knew about this responsibility I had assumed. Probably they would not have understood anyway.

Those of his stunts that were not disastrous sometimes appeared comical on the surface. But a layer of desperation often flowed beneath.

"The Night Dad Got The Cadillac Stolen," as my sisters and I named one episode, was in that category. He informed us of a plot to get his car stolen in order to collect insurance for a new one. It would be simple. He planned to leave the keys in the ignition and the garage door open. I considered it another of his jokes until the night someone backed the car out of our garage. I heard it accelerate and roar down the alley past our strawberry patch and a neighbor's giant weeds. Bam! Its crash into a light pole resounded through the rooms of our house.

I raced behind my father to the accident scene. He peeked in a car window and seemed oddly familiar with the curly-haired thief crouched on the floorboard. Neighbors in their bathrobes appeared, and a Mac policeman showed up to investigate. My father turned to me and said in a hushed voice, "See? It worked."

Even the unexpected addition of a canine to our family smacked of humor melded with duress. A strange bond existed between him and forlorn animals, especially dogs. Maybe it had to do with the puppy, Buddy, who Perry had bestowed on his young son in an uncharacteristically reckless gesture. Hattie, aghast at the prospect of potential germs or possible canine attacks, had banished the pet within hours.

So my father had established a habit of collecting stray dogs much like the down-on-their-luck people to whom he inevitably gravitated. It was as if they could curb his malaise. He was apt to rescue some forlorn or mangy animal from the street, let it ride with him in the Cadillac awhile, and feed it a morsel of food with a stream of conversation. Practically any dog or other specimen would do.

"How would you like to have a monkey?" he asked animal-loving Margo one day.

"Paul, have you lost your mind?" my mother exploded.

He ignored her and entertained "Snussy Puss" with the tale of his jailed client who owned a monkey named Gringo. He was so clever that he could curl his long tail through the jail bars. Maybe we could baby-sit Gringo until his client got out of the slammer, he suggested as my mother howled in protest.

One Saturday, he came into the kitchen pulling a shaky Dalmatian on a leash. "This is Spot. A fire engine dog," he announced. The terrified creature looked at us with one blue eye and a brown one before rushing to hide beneath the kitchen counter. "Her owner can't keep her, and she has nowhere to go," he said, appearing every bit as sad as the dog.

Margo, immediately smitten, begged to keep Spot.

"I know who will end up taking care of it. I will," my mother said, frowning. "It will be like having another baby."

After my father confessed that Spot's former home was a liquor store he had visited earlier that day, she was even more livid. But something caused her to relent, and Spot became a family fixture. My father began to joke about "being in the doghouse" after he had been naughty. And my mother lamented that she had five children to oversee – a trio of girls, a hapless dog, and a misbehaving husband.

There was a family code of silence concerning these canine adoptions, auto accidents, and other bizarre incidents. I was never to mention episodes like my discovery of a vodka bottle hidden in hollyhocks beside our garage either. My sisters and I were obligated to disclose nothing at all in public while smiling as if our father had already been elected governor. Already, our feet and psyches were rooted in two incompatible worlds.

Despite her ill view of politics, my mother collaborated with my father's ambitions to mold The Harem into those model daughters of political portraits. It did not occur to us that he should resemble other fathers and share in such a role. Though he showered us with affection in the form of wet kisses and head pats, most children seemed to baffle him. Small people affected him oddly, especially babies. When newborn Andrea had wailed, he seemed tentative about touching her. Feeding her a bottle or changing her diapers had been out of the question. Both were strictly "women's work."

He was seemingly fearful of alienating my sisters and me, and inevitably failed to carry out threats of punishment like spankings. Only once did he weaken and gently swat the behinds of Margo and me. Immediately, he apologized. "I love you. Do you love me, too?" So we just giggled and nodded our heads when Mom said repeatedly to her friends: "I've had to watch Paul grow up, you know. He is like having another child."

Her assigned task to transform The Harem to perfection was a challenge since our inclinations and temperaments were as disparate as our appearances. None of us appeared physically to belong to the same set of parents. As my father put it when strangers eyed us, "Mailman, maybe the milkman, stopped by once in awhile." It made me ponder the possibility that I might have been adopted as an infant and no one dared tell me.

My mother attached labels to our identities. She used them mainly when talking to acquaintances about us. It made me feel like we might as well be branded cattle.

She anointed Margo as "The Student." Her middle daughter had the Scandinavian look of wide blue eyes and wheat-colored hair surrounding a chubby face. She was a sturdy chunk of flesh who shunned dresses in preference of pants and wished she could be reincarnated as an animal. At various junctures, she had a guinea pig named Pete who squeaked for lettuce, Easter chicks who chirped incessantly, a black-and-white rabbit who hopped about the yard, a parakeet called Casey, a mallard duck who inexplicably appeared in our alley, and a turtle named Charlie who hid out in a bookcase. Razor smart and exceedingly ornery, Margo defied my mother to tame her.

Andrea was pronounced "The Cute One." She had come into the world with colic, freckles, a turned-up nose, and medium-red hair. Most of the time, she chose reticence over rambunctiousness. She looked to Margo for direction and tagged around after her, seemingly happy to be in her shadow. The first two years of life she had refused to talk and expected Margo to do it for her.

"The Role Model" was my designation. My appearance conjured my mother's dark eyes and brown hair, which she incessantly groomed. According to my father, I was beautiful. But my mother never said so. As the oldest, I was expected to be flawless and more accomplished than my sisters. She lectured me constantly about setting a good example for them. I was to entertain, baby-sit, shepherd, and monitor them. I led, and they were to follow. So, of course, they pronounced me bossy. They banded together to oppose me, making us a classic female triumvirate of rivals.

Each of us understood instinctively that our parents had singled out favorite children. It was not that any one of us got ignored or slighted. The favoritism was more subtle than that, and they would surely have denied it. My father had recruited me to his corner by wooing with adoring glances, and engaging in the political chatter that my mother disdained. He expected me to provide refuge when her cold shoulder emerged. His cheek tweaks and rotating eyes implored me to protect him against her rejection. When she refused to speak to him, I was the one to ferry messages between them. On occasion, that conjured my mother's hostility.

"You have more influence over your father than I do," she said more than once.

So Margo and Andrea were my mother's choices.

Though not exactly compliant, Margo seemed to have been born with a comforting nature. Even as a small child, she had been able to play the role of anchor when familial waters buffeted the rest of us. My mother gravitated to her when she needed to be soothed or understood. The older my sister got, the more she tried to shield Mom from the transgressions of her husband.

My sisters were inseparable, maybe because they shared a burlap-walled Walnut Street bedroom or for the simple reason that they were separated by just two years. All I knew for sure was that they often seemed a unit all their own, with their older be-a-role-model sister on the sidelines. I could only envy their bond.

Despite evident obstacles, Mom managed to corral us and transform The Harem ever so gradually into daughters who would not err should the opportunity arise. She never said so, but we understood that our father's political prominence implied a certain responsibility to present ourselves packaged as members of a Kodak-ready political family. She had us dress as if the photo shoot were imminent. We wore pretty pastel sweaters and shiny saddle shoes to school or expensive dresses paired with patent-leather shoes to church. We had Hattie to thank for such finery, purchased for us just as she funded my father's wardrobe.

My mother barked orders about standing up straight, saying "please" and "thank you," executing table manners, using the right words, grooming ourselves impeccably, and reams of other niceties. With her instructions, she issued observations such as, "It is more important that your children respect you than like you" or "Anything worthwhile is worth working for." She chose to bestow affection in the form of eti-quette tips and hand-ironed dresses instead of tender hugs or whispered endearments.

We balked at being perfect and feeling that each person encoun-tered represented a potential political vote for my father. But she was absolutely determined to complete her assignment. Sunday at the Congregational Church was our weekly showcase. Like it or not, we trotted dutifully down the center aisle behind our father. We smiled as his head bobbed from left to right and came to a halt when he stopped for an occasional handshake. No one needed to inform us that he might be there to honor the Lord but had hardly forgotten that political ballot casters might be lurking in the pews.

Of all our embarrassments, wearing clothes far fancier than our friends did, and riding in a Cadillac that artificially branded us as wealthy, ranked at the top. We longed to switch from being political mannequins to normal kids who did not need to impress anybody. Most of all, we wanted a regular father who stayed home.

The one day we could count on him being with us was Sunday. That was when we headed across town for our command performance visits to Hattie and Perry. It was a ritual so mandatory that doing so was not an option.

The Harem, Mom, and even Perry knew that we must endure the weekly three-act play to be performed there. It starred my father and Hattie. We were the audience. The plot was so familiar that I usually daydreamed through most of it while waiting for the conclusion of Act Three. It was the only important one.

En route across Mac, my father delivered his "DO NOT" lecture. The Role Model, The Student, and The Cute One sat in back with The Politician and Mrs. Anti-Politics up front. We waved at acquaintances in their yards while holding our arms stiffly to avoid hearty jerking as Mom had instructed. We offered subdued smiles that were not excessively cheesy.

The DO NOT spiel went something like, "Now be SURE not to mention in front of Hattie and Perry that we had company last night. Especially that any drinking went on. For God's Sake, DO NOT bring up anything about your mother buying new clothes or furniture either. And whatever you say, DO NOT mention Grandma Ida. You know how jealous Hattie is of her." He adjusted the rear view mirror to peer back at me. Catching my eye, he winked and said, "That especially goes for my Mrs. Sherlock Holmes, also known as Mrs. Tusswagon."

My mother was silent. The lovely smile she wore in church only a few hours before had vanished. Now she telegraphed her dread of the upcoming visit with a rigid jaw as my father aimed conversation away from her. Her face had that charcoal look, the one she wore every morning until coffee the texture of motor oil provided a jump start. Visits to Hattie seemed to render her near grievous and comatose.

Perhaps she was contemplating the acidic comments with which Hattie baited her. She might say, vinegar swishing in her voice: "My, that is a mighty fine looking handbag, Virginia. Pray tell, is it new?" Or "Mercy Sakes, Paul Andrew said your mother, Mrs. Teichgraeber, has another new car."

84

Puffing on a Pall Mall, my father would try to salvage the situation with a "Now Mama." But the poison would have already risen to settle between Hattie on her stool and my mother at her station next to the kitchen table, backed by faded floral wallpaper and yellowed drawn window shades.

It was one of the rare times when I understood how my mother might feel. It seemed to me that Hattie was no more fond of me than she was of my mother. She was not the kind of grandmother, like Grandma Ida, onto whose lap I would have considered climbing or asked to play a game of canasta. She would never have driven up to our Walnut Street curb and seen my sisters and me race toward her car with squeals of joy as we did when our other grandmother arrived. But then Hattie adamantly refused to learn how to drive. She seemed to regard us as inanimate objects. To her, we were not little girls who would welcome a hug or an invitation to sleep overnight. She had no upstairs dress-up closet where we could play, either, like Grandma Ida did. We were not even allowed to go to her upstairs. Instead, she just bought us things.

Even the way she looked was entirely different from my friends' grandmas. During our visits to Marlin Street, she sat on her kitchen stool and bore no resemblance to the Saturday Pegues Hattie. That was a lavishly garbed person whom we barely recognized. She wore extravagant hats piled with feathers and net, showy jewelry with red or amber stones, and gloves that smelled of moth balls and unused leather.

My father blamed the rheumatic fever she had contracted as a child for his mother's peculiarities. "She's a lil' 'tetched in the head," he said occasionally. "She can't help it."

I suppose that should have justified her countless trepidations. Besides her lengthy "Dangers List," there was the "Ailments List." Her erratic heartbeat must be connected somehow to indigestion, which might explain dull headaches and insomnia in a frail body whose blood did not circulate properly and whose bones ached. That did not include her frequent Spells.

"I'll be here next time you come, God willing," she liked to say. Another favorite was, "Just in case I should have gone into the beyond." Dying was one of her primary preoccupations. Sometimes I looked at her cadaver-white face and wondered whether she would vanish before our next visit.

I thought she was lucky that my grandfather was willing to tolerate peculiarities like her triple-locked doors, fantasies about invisible intruders, fears of leaving the house except to shop, and stockpiles of purchases that still bore price tags.

Perry did have his own set of odd habits though. Most of them involved being stingy, according to my father. He pulled his own teeth by affixing a string between them and a doorknob, bathed just once a week, had holes in his shoe soles, and never discarded food.

He kept all of his valuables in one kitchen corner opposite Hattie on her stool. Stacked in tidy piles across this counter were quantities of used rubber bands, folded brown paper sacks, fuzzy white pipe cleaners, paper clips, odd lengths of string, striped mints from restaurants, assorted pencil stubs and rusty nails. He sorted and rearranged his collections regularly. Near them, he kept a box of chocolate-covered cherries for "the girls," as he called us.

Unlike Hattie, Perry always looked exactly the same. Pipe in his hand. Shirt sleeves turned up two folds. Tie loosely knotted. Watch of imitation silver on his left wrist. Sweater of cardigan style and decidedly shabby. The only item that ever changed was his hat. Summer produced his battered straw one, and winter his tattered felt hat.

Each Sunday, when the Cadillac pulled onto the uneven concrete ribbon attaching Marlin Street with Perry's one-car garage, we saw a kitchen window shade lifted slightly. No face appeared, making it seem as if a ghost were behind it.

"It's Perry," my father said, turning off the ignition and unfolding himself from the car. Yet no one appeared as we stood like deserted soldiers on a concrete military base. As my father listened to keys rattle in each of the door locks that were lined up like vertical peepholes, he issued his ritual Sunday comment.

"Easier to get into Fort Knox than my own damned house," he said.

Once in the kitchen, the play began after obligatory "Hi, son, how are you?" and "Oh, Mama, you're looking pale" greetings had been exchanged. Act One of the production took place there. My father paraded back and forth past a table laden with spritz cookies, cherry pie and butter cake, and offered his most current political observations. Each visit featured a major announcement of some sort. It might concern a political coup or plum of a speaking engagement. "Freddie plans to … " he might begin. One hand swept thinning hair. He paused now and then to flick cigarette ashes into a crystal dish. "Word in the GOP is ... " These rumored confidences made his lips curl to resemble a satiated lion. They never seemed to cease moving. His words stretched toward infinity in the cadence of a 78 r.p.m. record that was revolving too slowly.

Hattie appeared riveted by his tour de force. Her head bobbed in concert to his verbal eruptions. His huge eyes drifted toward hers each time he passed her corner stool.

My stomach churned with sugar as steam hissed out of a heat grill. Though I longed to be somewhere else but there, I could sense his self-image as he carried on. I could visualize him sweeping across Kansas and standing before chanting crowds, a prophet-cum-evangelist who was destined to save his beloved state and all of his supporters.

As his hostage audience in a Marlin Street kitchen, we were powerless to resist the force of his ambition. He reminded me of an ocean wave that roared to our shore so regularly that its mighty sound had become a backdrop to our lives.

Act Two of the play had us adjourn to the living room. It was a dark place, entered only on Sundays, with a rug rolled at the base of its front door to obstruct possible intruders. Hattie, after her weekly "Never had a lesson in my life" proclamation, began to plunk out a rendition of "Beautiful Dreamer" on an upright piano in dire need of tuning. It prompted my father to lean on the French doors leading into the dining room. Aside from his silence and lack of a cigarette, he might have been reclining against the refrigerator in our kitchen. My sisters and I, who were in an advanced state of numbness by then, had devised a game to pass the time. Each of us tried to count how many fringed lamps, china figurines, porcelain dishes, lace doilies, and other knickknacks sat crowded together on tabletops and inside cupboards.

"Like growing up in a furniture store," my father liked to say. "Only Mama would never let me out of the kitchen."

After Act Two ended, Margo, Andrea, and I always compared our scores and speculated about whose names were Scotch-taped to the bottom of every item on paper scraps lettered in Hattie's shaky script. "To Cynthia with love from Hattie," one said. "For my darling Paul Andrew," said another. She had designated them in case she should travel "into the beyond." In all of her scribbling, though, she had neglected to reserve any of her precious possessions for Mom or Perry.

Act Three of the performance required that we follow her single file past the groaning tabletops, through the jampacked dining room with its pink wall telephone and breakfront crowded with fragile china, and back to the kitchen. We knew that our escape would come only after she climbed the creaky back hall stairs to enter a certain one of four bedrooms, each of them locked.

I had christened her destination "The Money Room" after the only occasion she allowed me upstairs.

"Be careful not to fall," she had cautioned on the way up through a dense aroma of moth balls where ghosts threatened to inhabit shadowy corners. "And promise not to touch anything."

With shaking hands, she had located the correct key from a weighty set of them to unlock a door. Finding it was not difficult because she knew these metal objects as intimately as the names taped beneath her figurines and bowls. Inside, the patterned wallpaper had reeked of stale perfume. Behind a bolted closet door hung rows of unworn suits and dresses with sales tags dangling from their pricey sleeves. Hat boxes filled with frothy concoctions stuck out beneath a big bed.

Mostly, the room had resembled a secret shrine to a small child. There were photographs of a baby with its head in a frilly bonnet and a ruffle about its neck, and one of it staring out from a wicker carriage. There was a portrait of a toddler in a floor length dress edged in lace, and another in a fluffy ensemble. I had thought maybe my grandmother had a daughter no one ever knew about until I noticed the inscription on one of the baby pictures: "Darling Paul Andrew."

This Money Room was where Hattie stashed the monthly cash proceeds from a wheat farm outside Mac that her father had given her. Some of these impressive sums, which Hattie called her "Wheat Money," financed the volumes of Pegues merchandise that she hid away and never wore. Most of it funded my father's silk suits, Cadillacs, and his other expenditures of which we were unaware.

To access her cash, Hattie had to locate another key and unlock the top drawer of a tall bureau. Inside were piles of unworn buttery leather gloves resting in elbow length cellophane wrappers. Their kaleidoscopic colors ranged from vivid red to chocolate brown, and sunflower yellow to grassy green. Beneath them she had hidden envelopes thickened by bills, and wrapped in fat rubber bands.

As she reached for them, her eyes had flown suddenly toward a dark window. "Someone has been in here, tampering with that window shade," she had shrieked. "Lord, a'Mercy."

We had fled, with Hattie in the lead clutching her envelope. Once back in the kitchen, my father had soothed his terrified mother while our own mother donned her "That's enough" expression.

After that, Hattie's presentation of her weekly bounty to my father might as well have been a Legion of Honor bestowal, considering its pomp. We had receded into the background as if invisible.

"Paul Andrew, this is for a little something. Famous politicians have to ... "

"Oh, Mama."

We had waited as the mutual endearments swirled and tightened a bond that sometimes seemed destined to strangle all of us.

* * * * *

Perhaps it was my mother's inevitable denigration of politics that caused my father to make his most contentious announcements in Hattie's kitchen. There she had to hold her tongue about those monster politicians who amounted to no good, a category into which she was tossing my father with alarming regularity.

So one Sunday we learned that his big news concerned Republican Governor Ed Arn, under whom Freddie was serving a second term as lieutenant governor. My father announced it in his special occasion bell-tolling voice. He told us that the governor, who hailed from Wichita, planned to travel all the way from his temporary home in Topeka to Mac. He was coming for dinner.

My mother began sputtering in response as Perry asked why on earth Governor Arn was journeying to Mac. My father ignored both of them to emphasize that Freddie was the connection, as usual. That news no doubt made my mother dislike him even more.

By the following day, though, she was rallying at full throttle for this occasion. She summoned her wealth of impressive domestic skills, which reflected her rigorous Kansas State University home economics training. She scurried about testing recipes written in her loopy handwriting, slathering woodwork and tabletops with lemon oil, laying clothing ensembles across her bed, experimenting with possible centerpieces for the table, and reprimanding The Harem that we had to behave by disappearing on the big night. It was an art already perfected during previous visits by political heavyweights.

"Children are to be seen, not heard" meant "Children are not to be seen OR heard" according to her interpretation.

On the big day, we choked down a round of late-afternoon peanut butter and jelly sandwiches. Then we were advised in no uncertain terms to vanish. So we did not get to see the car in which the governor arrived promptly at six o'clock. By then, we were crouching in our usual positions at the top of the front hall stairs in order to view the arriving guest.

I had devised a seating order. The top step, offering the optimum view, was mine. Margo and Andrea got the two steps below. I ignored their inevitable "You're SO bossy" complaints as we awaited our celebrity visitor.

Finally, the doorbell chimed. "WELLLL-COME, GUVVV-NER," my father boomed. We peeked through the spindles and struggled to see this important man. We had been told that he had already served on the Kansas Supreme Court and would no doubt be elected governor for a second term. I cranked my neck to get a better view. But all that my brief glimpse of him revealed from a skyward perch was the top of his head.

My mother, who was well on her way to being considered the Perle Mesta of Mac, had perfected every detail of such evenings. A compote supported by a slender stem of glass was filled with fat shiny balls and draped strands of beads. It sat at the center of her dining room table. China and silver and crystal, hand-rubbed with cotton towels, shone like reflective mirrors. Her dinner, warming in the oven, was a feast. It was timed for a seven o'clock presentation if she could coerce my father not to extend the cocktail hour, as he was wont to do.

Of course, most of Mac had been alerted to the governor's presence on Walnut Street. "Your dad is real important, isn't he?" a girl I hardly knew had asked me at school that day.

"What do you mean?" I was certain that her parents heard about THE visit from friends or neighbors, who probably listened in on someone else discussing it on a telephone party line and then told clerks at the grocery or hardware stores. Even the butcher uptown would have been informed that the governor of Kansas was about to visit Mac and the grand house of Paul Lackie. "You know, that Republican big shot who may be governor himself someday," one of them probably said. If a visit from the current governor was any indication, the odds looked pretty promising, the blabbing mouths of Mac were apt to have concluded.

Eventually, I would come to wonder what detour their conversations might have taken if one of them had been clairvoyant and able to predict my father's future.

Later that night, I awoke to the sound of words being hurled in voices fueled by vodka. Though I had never intended to be one of those snoopy kids who monitored adult behavior, I was becoming one. Some part of me yearned to understand who my mother was and how she got to be that way. I needed to sort out, too, the confusion about why my father flirted with me as if I were a political supporter or ravishing female and yet wounded me in ways it was premature to consider. Most of all, I wanted to comprehend why the fabric of my parents' relationship was becoming stained like a tablecloth with spilled red wine gradually infiltrating its whiteness.

She responded to his erratic behavior and political passions with a combination of cooperation and opposition. One day, she seemed to love and support him. "Snooky," he would say in gratitude, planting a wet kiss on her cheek.

The next day, she might oppose and belittle him. "Not the cold shoulder again, Virginia," he would plead before escaping to places where people would praise him.

Sometimes my mother, while offering enticing flattery followed by forbidding frigidity, made me think she possessed twin personalities like Hattie did.

Mom's verbal jabs made me ache for my father. I attempted to soothe him when the potency of her voice coerced him into rare silence. "It's going to be okay, Dad," I whispered out of her hearing. I tried to administer balm as if it could erase the marks her rage inflicted on both of us.

At first, her Walnut Street dream house had seemed to mellow her brittle edges. She had abandoned the inflammatory issue of my father siphoning her inheritance money from the bank and turned her frustrations toward something else that needed alteration. Using untapped sources of energy, she had tackled cavernous spaces to make them oases worthy of decorating magazine photos. She had outfitted them in tie-back muslin drapes edged with fringe, slip-covered the chairs to coordinate with sofas, placed handsome rugs over hardwood floors, and picked out unique antique pieces.

As if to court my father, she decorated their bedroom to resemble a cozy plaid cave. They napped there on Sunday afternoons behind a closed door, and emerged flushed afterward.

"Snooky, you is one dazzling dish," he would flirt later, rolling his marble size eyes.

Some noon hours, he arrived home for lunch. Afterward, they adjourned to red velour chairs in the parlor and shut the door to conduct "adult conversation." Such moments softened my mother's face and erased, momentarily, the memory of post-midnight clashes.

On Saturday nights, they trotted out in perfumed finery to star in the social firmament of Mac. She displayed a hairdo all fluffed and sprayed stiff at the beauty parlor. He carried a brown paper bag of booze in one hand. At the front door, he looked her over head to toe and called her a "clothes horse" or "a knockout." He swiveled his head left to right and winked at her.

In those days, he surprised her with gifts to enhance her glamorous image. The most memorable in my recollection was a pair of red leather stiletto high heels and a matching purse. He had brought them all the way from Kansas City and presented them in a spectacular pink box tied with red satin ribbon. "Ooooh, Paul ... " she had cooed at the sight of them.

When they flirted like that as if a pair of hormone-feverish adolescents, my heart lifted with happiness. "I wish I had parents like yours," my friend Becky said. No doubt, she was comparing them to her plump mother and milquetoast father. It required no imagination on my part to visualize my mom and dad as the governor and first lady of Kansas. I could see them riding in the back seat of an open convertible and waving at applauding crowds, as newspaper photos had sometimes depicted past governors and their wives.

I was not certain what a governor's wife did all day while her husband forged political deals and lunched with important people. But I knew my mother could apply her domestic genius to help plan those sumptuous official dinner parties like my father had attended and raved about. As first lady of Kansas, she could execute her exquisite table settings with one-of-a-kind centerpieces and delectable menus guaranteed to generate gushing thank-you notes. I thought Mom might be the finest governor's wife the Sunflower State ever had. The sole deterrent was her revulsion of politics.

Her "Look at what politics is doing to all of us" tirades made visions of my parents in a political motorcade, or at fancy Capitol dinners, fade. My heart turned to lead as their romantic waltz ground to a halt and became a tango choreographed amidst flying darts. I heard topics tossed that involved politics, booze, money, Hattie, more politics, and something about living in Topeka.

"What's wrong with having a normal life?" she petitioned him. The Harem could have a father who was on hand to answer homework questions or attend school plays. She could have a husband who helped out instead of a phantom who might as well not even live with us anymore.

"Everything about it is wrong this way," she complained, trotting out her list of specific grievances. All of the drinking in quantities that must ape his political cronies. So much money flowing out of Hattie's kitchen but never reaching our house. And by the way, where did all of that go? Couldn't he see that the political Freddies and Franks were conniving, dishonest, untrustworthy, egotistical, typical politicians? Especially Freddie, whom she had not trusted from the start. Didn't our family deserve the type of father and husband who preferred OUR company to theirs?

Her diatribes made me wish that politics would go away and make my mother smile again. Yet I knew that its absence would deflate my father and reduce him to someone none of us would recognize. She was right that a political life robbed us of him and left our household as if run by a single parent. It was true that he was never around to answer my questions about school assignments on history, a topic that was foreign to her. He had missed Andrea's recent school performance, too, causing her to weep that every other dad but him was applauding out front.

But surely my mother could see that his political passions fueled him as gasoline did a race car. Politics made him rev, recharge, rotate, and even race. It caused him to rise before dawn with a song on his tongue, spill words in endless streams, coerce the undecided to follow his logic, and sustain a dream whose light refused to be dimmed.

In the Fred Astaire and Doris Day movies whose Saturday matinee reels were my frame of reference for the way romance worked, lovers always found a way to end their disagreements and make up with smooches. But after each of my parents' battles, my mother's face got darker. The blacker it became, the less we saw of my father. He fled to places where people drank, acted silly, and relished life. I always imagined that he was at the Legion or VFW, swaying at the bar, until one Saturday afternoon changed all that.

* * * * *

While my mother was attempting to mold The Harem and my father was tearing about hell bent on his political goal, the family of Annas Brown had far different priorities. They were dedicating their time to achieving her release from prison.

Within three months of her incarceration, they had hired Hutch attorney Clair Hyter to seek her release. Somehow, Mrs. Brown's ex-husband John and their daughters Lucille and Juanita had managed to accumulate large quantities of money to help make it happen. Or perhaps their abortionist ex-wife and mother had amassed the funds from her "treatments" for which she reportedly charged $75 (nearly $600 today).

The Brown family quartet appeared to be rather savvy when it came to behind-the-scene politics and payoffs, too. They were privy to the fact that bribes could be offered and attorneys were not always honest. And they had no qualms about playing this game or even approaching government officials directly if it meant the prison release of Annas Brown.

Navy lieutenant Lackie poses in a California
yard with his stylish wife, Virginia, and their
daughter, Cynthia.

Kansas Governor Fred Hall testified that he did not receive
payoff funds related to Annas Brown's parole.

Abortionist Annas Brown (right) and her daughter,
Lucille Updegraffe, leave the Hutchinson courthouse
after her arraignment on manslaughter charges.
Photo courtesy of THE HUTCHINSON NEWS

Paul Andrew wears an unusually somber expression for his
official political portrait.

Aspirng governor Lackie watches as his wife, Virginia (to his left), greets well-wishers in the receiving line at a political soiree.

Perry, holding Margo, Hattie in one of her flamboyant hats, and Cynthia grace Virginia's floral living room sofa.

Virginia, holding Margo, with Cynthia.

The Lackie family, including Spot their Dalmatian, gathers for a newspaper photograph which appeared in the "Independence Daily Reporter."
Photo courtesy of INDEPENDENCE DAILY REPORTER

Virginia, who disliked being photographed, wore dark lipstick and an intricate hair style, which were fashionable in her youth.

Paul Andrew proved a dashing figure in his tilted Navy cap.

CHAPTER FIVE

A SEDUCTRESS IN PINK
1953

Vignettes from a woman's pink apartment began to tumble daily through my mind as I sat facing a classroom blackboard, gossiped with my friends about boys, or lay in bed unable to sleep. I saw the pink sofa. Pink plastic flowers. Pink printed curtains.

I looked at my mother, and a clamp clutched my heart.

Hard as I tried, I could not erase the memories of this pink place after my father took me there on one of our Saturday afternoon motor trips.

Our destination was out of Mac a ways to a blink-and-you-will-miss-it town with no Main Street. He presented this detour from our usual jaunt around Mac as a brief stop at someone's place to drop off political papers.

"Remember Josie?" he asked with studied casualness as we neared the end of our driveway. He flicked ashes in the Cadillac tray. "My secretary. She came to a party at our house last spring."

"I remember."

* * * * *

Josie had been a guest at one of the renowned buffet suppers hosted by my mother, who resembled an Indian maiden that night. The bodice of a yellow cotton dress had edged off her bronzed shoulders and its crinoline skirts bobbed above her delicate ankles. Her inky dark eyes had shone like deep pools.

She had bestowed upon me the unusual privilege of passing trays of crust-free miniature sandwiches among the guests who were scattered

97

across the wide front porch. Fearful that I might drop the tray or err in some other way, I was clutching it for dear life when someone had said, "Oh, here comes Paul. And who on earth is that with him?"

I had heard heels clicking across the concrete walk leading to the porch and cranked my head around to see. Blonde hair had drifted behind a face that God must have tried to make perfect. Her complexion had appeared to be without pores and was flushed with pale pink. She had been a monochromatic vision in a dress the color of creamy gauze with a skirt that swirled above high heels the same color. Only her earrings, which were the cornflower blue shade of her eyes, had not matched.

"This is Josie, my secretary." He had boomed it as if introducing a promising candidate at a political rally. His hand had rested at her diminutive waist.

"Hello," she had said with a small laugh that resembled the sound of wind chimes. She had seemed to float across the painted boards of our porch as if enveloped in an ethereal glow all her own. Her image had personified the celluloid and magazine movie stars I so admired.

"Whoa," some man near me had said in a loud whisper. "Paul's got a real prize this time."

My mother had come tearing across the porch to snatch the tray from my hands and say, "Time for you to go upstairs now."

Up in my room, I had sprawled across my bed and listened to voices travel onto the lawn where fireflies were flitting their yellow lanterns. Any other night I would have been out there with my sisters making the insects temporary prisoners in jars filled with hunks of grass or playing hide-and-seek. "ALL-EE, ALL-EE OXXXX IN FREEE!" I could hear us yell while drifting off to sleep.

Much later after the buffet guests had departed, I awakened to the sound of my parents in the kitchen. They were tossing nasty words at one another. Some of it had been muffled but not when Mom yelled, "It was your idea to invite Josie!"

As we set off in the Cadillac on that fateful Saturday outing, he said, "Well, then, you remember Josie helping me with all my political paper work. Couldn't do it without her, ya know, Mrs. Tusswagon." He reached over and patted my leg. "She's quite a gal."

Resentment tugged as he carried on about Josie. I did not care if she was a whiz with numbers who helped compute his political finances and sacrificed weekends to work Saturday mornings with him at the office. It mattered not to me that she was his most ardent gubernatorial supporter. All I knew was that a visit to her would ruin our afternoon together and make it slip away into that crevice where dashed opportunities got deposited.

"I have to deliver some important papers to Josie, some political stuff," he said. "She is convinced that I will be governor one day, ya know. She believes it every bit as much as I do." He stopped as if to let me digest that. "It'll just take a minute. Then I'll entertain you," he went on. "We'll go for a soda or something like I promised your mother. Okay?"

"Where does she live?" I watched the ugly scenery pass outside the window.

"Nortonville." That prompted another monologue about why she had decided to live in a tiny town 10 minutes from Mac because she was a farm girl who preferred rural scenery, how she had this talent for making an ugly apartment cozy, on and on. He kept chattering about her as we passed Free Methodist College, then the skeletal silhouette of National Cooperative Refinery Association equipment churning up and down to plumb for fuel, and finally into the country.

After awhile, he said, "Here we are." He turned off the main road and passed a couple of dismal-looking bars and a gas station. A few dogs hanging out on the street were the only signs of life. He pulled up in front of a two-story wood building. It was tidy but needed paint.

Narrow steps led up one side to a porch on the second floor. Josie must have been listening for the hum of the Cadillac. "It's my Tall Paul, the future governor of Kansas," she called in a singsong voice. She began waving from above but pulled back her hand at the sight of me.

"I've brought my other best girl." His eyes swept up to meet hers. Surprise etched small creases on her forehead as she looked at me.

"I'll wait in the car since it'll only take a minute," I said.

"No, Mrs. Tusswagon. You can't sit down here in the car all alone. Come on in. It won't take long." He clambered up the steps with me at his heels. At the top, he wrapped his arms around Josie and rocked her back and forth. She gripped his back with pointed pink fingernails. They were perfect and long instead of short and stubby like those of my mother. He muttered something about secretaries and bosses being friends before turning to wink my way.

"Welcome." She directed an incandescent smile at me and opened the screen door. She was even prettier than I remembered. Pink barrettes held her fluffy hair away from the milky face, and her eyes matched a flawless sky. She reminded me of a Swedish angel.

Pink was how I would remember her ever after. She wore it top to bottom in shorts, halter top, earrings, toenails, lipstick. It made her become color coordinated with her living room and kitchen. Even her throw rugs were pink.

It was the color my mother disliked most. She would not allow a trace of it in our house. I could imagine her appraising Josie's junky living room and squinting her eyes with one of her "You can't buy taste" verdicts.

My father moved past the couch to a little table with pink place mats and two straight chairs beside a door into the kitchen. He picked up a half full bottle of vodka and poured into two empty glasses.

"Wait a minute." Josie hurried into the kitchen. Ice cubes crackled as they left a tray. She rushed back carrying a plastic ice bucket in one hand and a glass of lemonade in the other. "You can sit here and drink it." She directed me to one of the chairs.

"Let's sit on the couch, Tall Paul." She walked toward it with bare feet prowling across the carpet like a graceful gazelle. She was curved and smooth all over.

His eyes followed her and messaged that he wanted to touch her. He sat beside her and lighted a cigarette instead. His hands trembled as he cupped the flame.

"I'll have one, too," she said, bending close so he could light it.

"Have you heard the one about ... ?" Suddenly he was rattling off jokes in slapdash fashion. He could not seem to tell them fast enough. His words piled up in layers coated with her infectious laughter.

"Oh," she tittered and touched his leg. They locked eyes. I looked away, frozen to the chair and aching to escape a room where I did not belong. I wanted to ask him, "When are you going to bring up politics?" so we could get it over with and leave.

"Cynthia?" He looked my way as if plumbing my thoughts. "Why don't you go outside and get some fresh air? Walk about a little bit or something?"

Or something? First, he would not let me sit in the car. Now he wanted me to leave. I got up and moved toward the door. Was I supposed to go hang out on the sidewalk with a pack of Nortonville dogs?

Outdoors, tears stung my eyes. I tried not to cry but could not seem to stop. My throat felt clogged and stuffed with pain. I considered walking out to the highway and hitching a ride to Mac. Other kids I had seen along roads did that. They pointed thumbs to the sky or held crudely lettered cardboard signs. Mine would read "MCPHERSON." But where would I get the cardboard? Besides, my father had always made nasty slurs about hitchhikers and the dangers they might encounter.

I walked up and down the empty street. No little kids were out playing or cars driving by. Even the dogs, except for one sleeping at the curb, had vanished. What was I going to tell Mom when she asked if we had a nice afternoon together? How was I supposed to respond when she inquired about where we had gone? The questions hammered my forehead like a migraine headache.

101

It would be impossible to answer quite casually, "We stopped by Josie's house" or "Dad had some political business to take care of with his secretary." I could not tell her about the visit unless he did. If she found out, she would be furious at me for agreeing to go instead of exiting the car on our driveway. She would yell at my father, too, and accuse him of seeking out another beautiful woman. The feeling of being crunched in the middle between them washed over me once again.

After what seemed like hours out on the sidewalk, I decided to start back up the steps. I stomped down hard on each one to warn them of my arrival.

Opening the screen door, I squinted in the dark as sunspots danced across my eyes. As my vision began to clear, I jerked at the sight of Josie and my father stuffed in a corner of the couch. She sat on his lap sideways with her legs flung across the cushions. Her hair stuck out of its barrette on one side and was still swept back on the other. It made her blotchy face look lopsided. She grasped a dangling strap of her halter. Flesh threatened to flow from it.

My father wore a wild look in his eyes and lipstick smeared across one cheek. "Time to go!" He nearly tossed Josie to the floor in his haste to rise. Then he mopped perspiration on his forehead with a handkerchief my mother had pressed on her mangle iron.

Josie stammered, "Cynthia, you must come back and visit again soon. Your daddy talks about you so much, you know."

"Go on down now," he said, gesturing vaguely. "I'll be there in a minute."

In the car, my tears puddled again. Fuzzy memories beat against my heart and tried to crystallize. Something set off fragments from my parents' battles when my mother and I had visited his California Navy base. The vignettes advised me that I already knew about my father and women like Josie.

* * * * *

102

"How could you do that to me?" she had yelled at him in California. Then she had mentioned an unfamiliar woman's name and something about a letter he sent her in Mac. Whimpers like the sounds of a wounded animal had escaped her throat as she stormed about his loving someone else.

I had listened as she blurted fragments from his letter. "Met her on the train. Did not mean to hurt you. Love her. War changes things. Divorce. You wrote me that you wanted a divorce." She had wept with heaving sobs as if her heart was splintering.

More tears had spilled as she mentioned a baby boy, who had lived long enough in her womb to reveal his sex before terminating his nine-month formation. I had no recollection of it, and would not hear him referred to again. My unborn brother had been relegated to the dark cavern of family unmentionables.

My mother and I had boarded a Mac train bound out of Perry's depot to the land of sunshine and movie stars. As we had pulled out of the station, I sat next to the window waving at him until his body was just a tiny speck. Already, I missed him but was too excited about seeing the Pacific Ocean to cry.

On the train, men in military uniform had milled all about us. One of them had come to sit down across the aisle. My mother had introduced him to me in that voice with a smoky drawl, which no one who heard it ever forgot. She had worn shiny red nail polish, a short skirt advertising those "Teichgraeber legs," and a radiant lipstick smile.

The soldier had escorted us to the club car and ordered a pink concoction with a maraschino cherry for me and something much stronger for them. He had sat very close to my mother and touched her now and then. After another round of drinks, she had begun to return his gestures.

Memory tells me that the soldier never left us after that. He had hovered nearby day and night until the train pulled into the California station. Outside the filmy train window, I had seen my father waiting.

103

Standing near a palm tree, he had loomed as a figure more dashing than I remembered. When we had stepped down into his arms, he bathed us in wet kisses.

"Snooky" and "Tooie," he had murmured. "Oh, my darlins'." This was the lovesick soldier who had cooed in letters to my mother: "Ya knows I loves ya boogsiest of everyone in the world." He had signed them "Your Paul."

After their ugly battle, I must have tried to overlay that scene with sweeter ones. I had chosen to remember my father crooning at my mother and coaxing her to smile back at him. I had treasured his flirting glances at her that were destined to generate electricity.

My mind had stored memories of strolling barefoot on warm sand beside the swollen ocean. He had held her hand as I skipped a zigzag path in front of them. Later, someone had snapped our photo in a sunny front yard. I had stood between my parents, each of them holding one of my hands. My father had looked patriotic and statuesque in his military ensemble, and my mother exuded style in a svelte dress and oversized picture hat. She had pinned a fat white bow atop my dark hair. My parents had squinted in the blinding light, perhaps from pensiveness.

* * * * *

"So, my Mrs. Tusswagon," my father said, jerking open his car door outside Josie's apartment. His stare penetrated the left side of my face. "SOOOO. What would you like to do on our special afternoon together?" He turned the key in the ignition and reached over to jiggle my cheek.

"I want to go home."

"Home? Now, darlin', this was to be our special time. Just you and me. You aren't upset that I stopped by Josie's for a minute, are you?"

"I thought you had important political papers to deliver."

"Well ... I just decided to talk with her about those matters instead of bringing along a stack of papers."

"I didn't hear you talk about it."

"We, uh, did it while you were outside."

Memory fails to reconstruct the rest of it precisely. Somehow we made the journey from Nortonville to Mac. He talked but I did not pretend to listen. My heart soared with tender images of his exulting at my first-place prize as Joan of Arc wearing tin foil armor in Mac's annual All Schools Day parade. Then it crashed at the indelibly etched image of him on the couch with Josie. Other vignettes and memories blurred together to gang up on my heart and shred it. I felt heavy and tired as if a weight had fallen into my stomach to hold me down. It made me want to vomit. My eyes burned with the pain of knowing that I would never again see my father exactly the same as before.

As we neared Walnut Street, he offered some version of "No need to mention to your mother where we went this afternoon. This is our lil' secret, Mrs. Tusswagon, just between you and me."

Lying to her. That was what he expected of me. He wanted me to fib to the person who lectured constantly that "People always find out if you lie" and "The truth is best even if it hurts." He was treating lying as if it were ordinary and common, just a simple dilution or even reconstruction of facts. His assumption that I would cover for him to help smooth the torturous marital tango that he and she had begun to dance enraged me. It also made me wonder whether this was how politicians conducted business, and if it was the reason Mom disliked them.

I toyed with the idea that my mother suspected his ugly secret. Maybe that explained why she was lying in a dark bedroom some afternoons when we came home from school or broke into tears for dumb reasons. Perhaps Josie was the reason she flew into rages about Margo's dirt spots on a freshly laundered choir robe or my forgetting to make my bed. Maybe that explained why she shot him resentful looks about Saturday mornings at his office.

I considered whether it could somehow be our fault that he was seeking comfort at a pink apartment. Maybe something my sisters and

I were doing was the cause of his flight. Yet I could not think what it might be. All I knew was that he seemed to want a secret life no one in the family was supposed to know about except me.

Resentment and hurt sent blood rushing through my throat and up onto my cheeks. "Don't do this. Don't put me in the middle between you and Mom," I wanted to scream at him. "Don't make me lie for you." Yet I could not force myself to talk to him about what I had witnessed. My 13-year-old voice lacked the confidence to confront him. I only wanted to pretend that we had never stepped into that pink apartment, that my father would not do anything to wound my mother, and that he could not be the kind of dad who wore someone else's lipstick smeared across a cheek.

Late that night, I lay in bed staring at black nothingness. Images of my father's flushed face, Josie's bared chest, her lipstick on his cheek, and his hands wrapped around her waist tumbled through my mind like clothes in a rotating dryer. I shut my eyes tight and willed tears not to trickle down onto my pillow. "I love you, Snooky," I could hear him say to my mother. "Do you love me, too?"

Was it possible that I could be mistaken about what I had seen? Maybe he was just playacting a romantic role with Josie to show her his dramatic skills. It was my mother he truly loved even if Josie was prettier. He could not be cruel enough to deceive her like that. My hopeful heart began thumping a little less.

* * * * *

The Monday morning after that, he leaned against the refrigerator as usual. His lengthy toilette had been completed. Fragrance wafted across the kitchen to the counter where my sisters and I sat. I stared down into my cereal bowl and worried that I might burst into tears.

"So what's on the agenda at school today, girls? Mrs. Tusswagon, why don't you tell us first?"

106

"I ... " My head remained bent.

"School ain't all that grim, is it?" He snickered.

"I have a stomachache." I sensed my mother listening even though she stood at the stove with her back to us. She hated everything about early morning and rarely talked until caffeine made her rally.

"Bet a lift to school would make your stomach feel better. Anyway, it's raining."

"No ... I'll ..."

"Would you like to ride in my beautiful balloon?" He swished a hand toward the back door.

"Just because Hattie walked you to school with an umbrella, you don't have to ... "

My father examined my mother's turned back, cleared his throat, and said, "Mrs. Tusswagon, your chariot is waiting."

In the Cadillac, I huddled next to the door handle and hoped he would not reach out to pat some part of me. He hummed as if that would clear away the tension hanging between us. I tried to connect the person behind the steering wheel with the one in Josie's apartment. His voice sounded the same as before. He seemed as sunny as ever. It was as if nothing had ever occurred. Perhaps he didn't realize what I had observed or think that I was old enough to suspect the intimate behaviors of amorous men with beautiful women.

"Here we are." The Cadillac glided to a stop near my school's front door. "Have them call your mother if that stomachache doesn't get better."

I stabbed at the door handle, suddenly aware that my hands were quivering. As I was halfway out the door, I heard, "I love you. Do you ... ?"

I shut the car door. Guilt threaded through my veins. I turned to wave at him. He blew me a kiss.

Probably he could not have fathomed, even if I had summoned the courage to tell him, that a single Saturday afternoon transformed me from a trusting girl to someone else whose eyes would be forever wary.

* * * * *

Like Josie, Annas Brown would no doubt have been thrilled to live in a pink apartment. Even a purple, orange or scarlet one would probably have been preferable to the stark concrete and barbed wire of the Kansas Industrial Farm for Women.

By the first month of 1954, this had been her home for just over three years. During that time, she had exchanged street clothes like her favorite beige suit for drab prison garb.

The females with whom the abortionist lived, ate, and slept daily were as grim as her surroundings. Some of them may also have been ill with syphilis or gonorrhea. Since World War I, women diagnosed with venereal diseases had resided at the Lansing prison.

During that war, sexually transmitted diseases being spread by prostitutes had become a significant problem in Kansas. So the legislature passed a 1917 law called Section 205. The legislation authorized imprisonment at the State Industrial Farm for Women of females who carried the diseases. Ever since, they had shared quarters with incarcerated women.

The daily prison activities of wartime inmates had included learning and performing household duties, doing laundry and kitchen work, and running the farm and its dairy. The theory was that these acquired skills might benefit the prisoners after their release. Unfortunately, the notion did not prove to be foolproof. Many of the women, once released, returned to prostitution anyway.

Now Annas Brown was keeping company with some of them. Not until 1956, a year after she was paroled, would this prison quarantine law be rescinded.

CHAPTER SIX

THE FATEFUL INQUIRY
Early 1954

"You'll never believe who has invited himself for dinner," my father crowed to us in the kitchen. He vibrated with the energy that promised some outrageous deed.

"Ike," I said, half believing that it was possible.

"NOOOOOO, Mrs. Tusswagon. And it's not the Pope either."

"Roy Rogers," Margo said.

"And Trigger?" asked Andrea.

"WELLLL. You're all wrong. FREH-DDDDDDEEE. Freddie, the lieutenant governor of this fine state of Kansas. That's who."

"Whaaaat?" My mother's voice resembled a reedy pitch pipe. "And Leadell, too. It must be something important to bring them all the way to Mac."

"His WIFE is coming?" My mother wore panic scratched across her face as if a stylus had maimed her.

He wandered off into reassurances that Freddie was not a fussy eater and she need not worry about the menu. As for Leadell's food preferences, he could not say. But one thing was sure. Freddie had made a genuine catch when he snagged her. A "real looker," that Leadell, he said.

My mother might as well have been preparing for the arrival of Ike or the Pope as she raced about testing menu choices from recipe cards strewn across the kitchen counter, resetting the dining room table with a rainbow assortment of candles and centerpieces, rearranging living room furniture, and dusting under and inside sofas and chairs. Though she disliked Freddie intensely, she was not about to jeopardize her Perle Mesta reputation.

109

On the momentous night of the visit, my sisters and I huddled at the top of the front hall stairs. We might have been a trio of perched birds, forbidden to fly or chirp.

"WELLLL," my father said, rushing to fling open the door when the bell chimed. "WHYYY, LEEE-UH-DELLL, AREN'T YOUUU THE PURR-TEE-UST THANG."

I grazed the top of Margo's head below mine and stuck my nose through the stair spindle in an attempt to glimpse Leadell. All I could see was the top of her head. I longed to shout, "Hi," so that she might look up our way. But she was so busy giggling in concert to my father's flattery that she might not have heard it even if uttered. He extended a bony hand to shake that of Freddie and droned on until my mother issued an invitation for drinks in the parlor where embroidered cocktail napkins awaited.

My sisters, who did not seem to share my level of interest in celebrity political visitors, got up and left for their bedroom. I lingered, yearning to possess hearing so acute that I might eavesdrop on the parlor conversation occurring over clinking glasses. I imagined that my father and Freddie, as cronies who spoke the same jargon, were weaving political stories around each other. It seemed to me that banter should be easy between pals who shared a common goal. After all, the state of Kansas and its highest office were supposed to belong to each of them before long.

About to follow my sisters' retreat, I heard the rat-a-tat of my father's words move toward the dining room. I could envision my mother in a state of composure by then as she led her guests to a table that evoked the governor's mansion on a politically star-studded night. She was advertising her exemplary posture and swaying only slightly from the headiness of entertaining a lieutenant governor coupled with euphoria that a healthy swig of vodka could produce. She was on her own turf. It was one that my father could not steal. Only Mom could excel in this world she had created away from his.

BOOM! A noise reverberated up the stairs from the kitchen.

"WHOO-ee! Never a dull moment." My father was bellowing as his footsteps raced through the dining room door into the kitchen. He laughed with one of his forced versions, which echoed like a megaphone. "WHOO-ee. Fine time for the coffeepot to explode!"

He had to be referring to our only coffeepot, the glass one that sat on the stove top and sent brown bubbles percolating through its clear stem. It, and the rest of dinner, was being monitored by our faithful "Mar-EEE The Menn-OH-nite." Or so my father called the pious-faced Mennonite girl who assisted Mom on special occasions.

* * * * *

The following morning, he offered a dramatic account of the glass pot exploding and sending shards shooting like rocket fire all about the kitchen. He made a valiant attempt to lift my mother's morose mood by turning this flaw in her culinary performance into a joke. Nothing like a little fireworks to keep things lively, he bantered. After all, where else would a lieutenant governor experience such kitchen pyrotechnics?

But he had much more significant news to deliver to us that morning. It was so monumental that he did not even save it for Hattie's kitchen.

"Freddie plans to run for governor," he said, pausing as if awaiting clashing cymbals. Just think of it! Freddie heading the almighty Sunflower State. And GUESS who he had asked to serve as his campaign manager! He puffed with pride like a magician who had just produced the proverbial live rabbit. He waited until Margo finally delivered the expected line.

"You, Dad?"

Exactly right, he said, jiggling her cheek. He ignored my mother, who was smoking a cigarette off in the corner and wearing her Wicked Witch of the Midwest face.

* * * * *

The next announcement, within days, circumvented Hattie again.

"I'm getting an apartment in Topeka," he said nonchalantly from his breakfast time position in the kitchen. He was resplendent in a starched white shirt and Countess Mara silk tie. Pall Mall smoke drifted above him to pool near the ceiling. The Town House Apartments, he said, drawing out the town part. That was the name of his new state capital residence. He coursed on with vague descriptions of it until my mother interrupted.

"Paul. I thought we were going to tell them later, after Hattie and Perry."

He flipped the hand not encumbered with a cigarette to shoo away her comment and looked our way. "Girls, now don't get the wrong idea. Mr. Pops is not moving out." He grinned as if we should be relieved that he would be living with us part of the time.

The following Sunday, en route to Marlin Street, he neglected to include the Topeka apartment topic in his DO NOT lecture.

In Hattie's kitchen, he prattled on about big happenings at the Capitol. When he paused, Margo piped up, "Mr. Pops, you forgot to tell Perry and Hattie about your new apartment."

He suppressed a gasp before glaring at her. Then his eyes began their rotation toward the ceiling, over the porcelain sink, across ancient wallpaper, and down to tired linoleum.

"An APARTMENT? In Topeka?" Perry removed his pipe to clamp jaws together like vices. "Paul Andrew, how can you afford ... ?"

"Leave the child be." Hattie cut him off. Why, famous politicians had to conduct business somewhere, she said. No trace of surprise tinged her voice.

My father rewarded her with a grateful smile before launching into diversionary political observations about Ike and his "She looks older than the mother of God" wife Mamie.

112

Once we were back in the car, he berated Margo. How in God's name could she bring up his apartment?

She appeared startled at hearing a father who never yelled or even raised his voice do both. Finally, he lowered his decibels and began offering sketchy details about the apartment. Margo looked even more bewildered. She was witnessing, once again, his cunning ability to chatter nonstop about a mystery like this place in Topeka as if fully informing us. Yet we would know as little about it by the time he finished as at the start. The bottom line was that straight explanations were not in his repertoire.

My mother, who had brooded silently through the Marlin Street tension, erupted in the front seat. "It's not right for you to expect these girls to lie for you, Paul," she said before spinning off into comments about her efforts to teach us right from wrong.

As they sparred, I struggled to visualize this place my father would live and sleep at night away from us. He had described it as a simple room. Nothing fancy. Bedroom and bath. A place to make phone calls. Or maybe hold political meetings.

I supposed that he would line its bathroom counter just like the one at home. There would be cologne, shave cream, one razor for his face and another for armpits, deodorant, scented soap, and all the other necessities to perform his toilette. He was apt to unload the contents of his Cadillac trunk, too. It resembled a traveling home with a typewriter, accordion files, typing paper, cartons of cigarettes, road maps, phone books of various towns, an ice chest, and bottles in brown paper bags. "Missed my calling. Should a' been a traveling salesman," he liked to joke about his portable residence in a car trunk.

I wondered whether Josie would travel to this new apartment. My skin prickled whenever I thought of her. My father's secret, which was now mine, too, had begun to stalk me. At unexpected moments, I envisioned him on the couch with Josie or heard her tinkling laugh.

I wondered whether he could possibly love two women at once. My naivete about such matters prevented a full examination of the question. So I studied my parents for clues. They hugged and kissed. He pinched her cheek and called her Snooky. Sometimes he could still make her face turn from sour to sweet. I could not fathom that he could be like this with her and then turn into a person who got another woman's lipstick smeared across his face.

It did not occur to me to deposit all of my conflicted emotions about him and Josie in another person's ears. I had hoarded my father's secrets for too long to spill them. Somewhere during his early courtship of me, perhaps when I was five or six, I had been anointed his keeper of confidences. His "This is just between you and me" and "There's no need to tell your mother" admonitions had slowly snowballed into blind collusion with him. So I carried the Josie deception buried inside with all the others. Yet every once in awhile, the sham of her and him separated from the rest and seeped into my heart. There it clouded my world with bruising purples and blacks.

Maybe that was what made my suspicions cluster around his reasons for getting this apartment. Fathers of my friends never traveled at all unless a business trip took them away for one night. So they had no familiarity with a dad who announced his looming part-time residency off in a distant city. I could not imagine trying to explain to them why my father was so different from theirs and had to live somewhere else part of the time, even if he was a politician. Maybe I should tell them that we were kind of like the Harry Truman family had been when he was U.S. Senator, with wife Bess and daughter Margaret residing across the border from us in Missouri half of every year while their politician lived in Washington, D.C.

Topeka, the capital of Kansas and my father's new temporary residence, sits west of Kansas City lodged between towns with confounding names like Tonganoxie and Paxico. It is also fairly near the community of Lansing with its Industrial Farm for Women and the federal prison in Leavenworth.

Despite 80-mile-per-hour speed limits, my father would have to spend at least three hours traveling each way between Mac and Topeka to help Freddie defeat his Democratic challenger. He was a banker from Lawrence named George Docking.

Freddie had already demonstrated considerable political clout by emerging victorious in a gubernatorial primary election. His opponent had been George Templar, a former state senator who enjoyed the support of most key newspapers. The senator had even garnered the backing of Governor Arn. That was an overt insult to Freddie, who had been his lieutenant governor for two terms. But the pair had spent much of their political alliance in open conflict. Governor Arn was apparently not the only one who considered Freddie difficult. Kansas historical records would later describe him as "a trouble maker" and "overbearing."

The gubernatorial campaign slogan that was to drive Freddie's bid, and be bellowed across Kansas, smacked of my father's bent for dramatic impact:

"LET'S CLEAN UP TOPEKA AS PRESIDENT
EISENHOWER HAS CLEANED UP WASHINGTON"

With that as their rallying cry, he and his candidate began to crisscross Kansas. They appeared at church suppers and civic festivals in towns with names like Junction City and Great Bend. Every now and then, my father stopped at home in Mac and regaled us with political tales. He brought newspapers from communities we had never heard of. We were supposed to be interested.

Perhaps it was the campaign slogan that sent my father into a frenzy when he learned that Ike, as proud Kansans called him, was to visit his home state for a parade. He announced that we must attend and wear flag colors, sending my mother into a frantic attempt to outfit us. She even shed her apathy toward politics and equipped us with small American flags to wave.

115

On Parade Day, we practiced with our flags fluttering out the Cadillac windows as my father sang "God Bless America" or rattled on about Ike and Alf Landon, a Kansas presidential aspirant. He had assigned both to his repertoire of supposedly close political pals.

Along the parade route, throngs of shouting loyalists carried "We Like Ike" banners or other homemade salutations. After what seemed an interminable wait, I began to wish my father was like my friends' dads who had never insisted on such a political outing. How important could it be to get crushed in a crowd just to watch someone go by and wave from a car?

Then sudden cheers broke out. People jumped up and down. My sisters and I sneaked through the legs of adults in front of us to get a peek at Ike. There he was, flashing his wide grin. "We like Ike!" we shouted. I looked at my father, whose face was flushed with joy.

Years later, Margo reminisced about the euphoria of it all and our father's exultation: "Dad opened up the world to us, doing things like taking us to see Eisenhower."

* * * * *

By late spring, he seemed giddy concerning his brilliant political prospects as a tag-along candidate after Freddie. Perhaps in celebration of his expanding prominence, or to refresh our memory that we still had a dad, he shocked us by proposing a family vacation.

My sisters and I had no familiarity with such an event. Every summer, we had watched our friends depart for destinations that boasted bodies of water other than a public pool or were famous sites like the nation's capital. My suspicion had always been that we never took vacations because our parents did not engage in physical recreation of any sort. Neither of them could swim. He considered walking from our house to the garage sufficient exercise. And my mother, who had abandoned horseback riding after getting tossed onto the ground and injuring her head, expended all of her spare energy on housework.

"Hollyyyy-WOOD!" he proclaimed. That was where we would travel. It would require driving for three days and crossing the desert in August without air conditioning.

* * * * *

We set off one dawn headed due west. We were prepared to be bored by Kansas scenery as familiar as our names. Silos, barns, cows, horses, wheat fields, hay bundles, combines, tractors, and flatness stretched toward infinity. By late morning, The Harem rode with bare feet hanging out the back windows while bodies were jousting for space on the scalding seat.

"You're in my way." Margo shoved Andrea with her foot.

"Owwww."

"Stop fighting RIGHT now" came from the front seat. "Did you HEAR me?"

My father, who was preoccupied with talking and singing along with a country western radio station, ignored us. He adored all those sad tales of splintered hearts from love gone awry and wayward souls who found solace in a bottle. The rest of us despised country music, but he said the driver got to choose. Across Colorado, he talked and sang and smoked until his voice got hoarse.

On the second day as we neared Salt Lake City, I made a request. "I want to see the Mormon Tabernacle. Please, can't we?"

He cleared his throat. I could sense him rehearsing. "Soooooo?" Had he heard me say I wanted to see a shrine to that so-and-so Joseph Smith, righteous soul he was of all those upright Mormons? Of course, the part about all those wives didn't exactly fit, did it? Bunch of hypocrites they were. "BIG-uh-ME!" he shouted. "More-MUNNNNN."

"PUH-LEEEEZ," I begged.

"Mrs. TUSS-wagon. You are SO dramatic. You should be on the stage." He paused before delivering the rejoinder we all knew was coming.

117

"I know. The last stage coach out of town," I finished. "Please ... "

"Noooo." He waved a hand goodbye in the direction of Salt Lake City. "I think what I need instead is a nice stiff drink. Yes, a drink I think."

Once we had arrived in the land of movie stars, he decided against looking up his distant cousin Dennis who had sped out of Mac on a motorcycle after high school. His intent had been to seduce Hollywood. But he had ended up cleaning actress Jayne Mansfield's heart-shaped swimming pool. Still, his tale of flirting with fame remained a topic of gossip in Mac.

We would visit a Roy Rogers movie set instead of Dennis. That meant seeing his horse, Trigger, too. This announcement prompted Margo, who had long begged my father to get her a horse, to reach out and pat his cheek.

She hardly suspected that her dream would soon come true with the unexpected acquisition of a horse named Gypsy. Like George-the-Gardener, the animal would arrive under mysterious circumstances. His owner, my father's law client, was a cowboy called Bobby Joe. He was destined to visit our house one night wearing an enormous felt hat, a shirt with hanging strings, and boots with silver spurs and turquoise stripes.

After Bobby Joe left, my father would summon Margo to offer a roundabout explanation of why she suddenly possessed a horse. This cowboy fellow's wife had run off with a rodeo character and left Gypsy behind, he would say. The horse reminded a bereft Bobby Joe of her so much that he couldn't stand the sight of it anymore. "Owes me some money," he would add, ignoring my mother's objections about how in the world we could take care of a horse.

So Margo was transfixed as we stood on the Hollywood set looking at Trigger hitched to a post. We stifled impressed gasps as Roy walked out onto a fake Western street. His face was crinkled, and he wore a Stetson just like on the movie screen in Mac. He bungled his lines, over and over. In between takes, makeup technicians rushed up to swab his perspiring face.

Roy seemed to sense that we were watching him because he waved farewell as our tour group started to exit. It prompted my father to run over, shake his hand, and introduce himself as a Kansas politician who would probably be governor one day soon. Roy had no way of knowing that he was in the process of joining that select first-name circle of his celebrity friends.

* * * * *

Since my father flirted with danger nearly as intensely as with women, perhaps those ornery gods of politics had orchestrated his coupling with Annas Brown after our return from Hollywood. They must have devoted careful planning to ensure that Perry would be located at a site where he would be forced to deal with someone who represented the abortionist. It was a coincidence that would place his son and a murderess in fateful juxtaposition.

Perry had retired recently from a lifetime of work for the railroad. For strings of numbing days, which had turned into many years, he sold tickets in a depot of air putrid from smoke and the noise of kids running across wood floors. His daily work routine had been as predictable as the route of his Packard to Hutch.

Each morning, he had dipped Hattie's homemade Swedish rusks into coffee percolated with a raw egg. Then he had locked her up inside their house and walked three blocks to work. He had departed daily at precisely the same time. During his absence, she had crocheted edges on towels, stitched squares for quilts, or ironed shirts for which he paid her two cents each. For companionship, she had turned to radio soap operas and drifted off into the tempestuous love affairs of their stars.

Late each afternoon, he had followed his same route back to their worn frame house. Over the railroad tracks. Past the city block-size park. Around the corner past two houses. Into their narrow driveway. After they had consumed dinner at their kitchen table, he tossed chicken bones or potato peelings into his special coffee can and dumped them behind the garage. Later, they went to sleep upstairs in the bed her parents had bestowed as a wedding gift. They moved through life together in some sort of numbed lock step. At least, it seemed so to me.

Shortly after Perry's retirement began, it became as monotonous as his railroad days and married life. And it was even less fulfilling. Hattie asked him to rush to the grocery store for powdered sugar or a bottle of cream. She requested his help hanging laundry on the basement clotheslines or needed assistance with the vacuum cleaner. She also expected him to listen full time to the news of oncoming Spells or her Disasters List.

Perry, who had never traveled farther than Illinois, entertained youthful dreams of visiting the ocean and viewing mountain peaks. His ambition had come close to materializing when the railroad offered him a job in the West. But his wife would not hear of it. Uprooting a boy like Paul Andrew might damage him, she had insisted. No, it was out of the question.

So he had gradually abandoned illusions about a life beyond Mac and sights other than farm land. Eventually it had caused him to conjure the question, "Why would anybody in their right mind want to live anywhere but Mac?" Yet retirement was prompting a new restlessness in him.

One Sunday, during a lull in conversation, Perry asked my father, "Do you suppose your friend, Freddie, would know of a job of some sort for me?"

"YOU?" My father's eyes rolled as Hattie's swept to her outstretched feet.

"Yes."

"Sure, Dad, I suppose. As I've said, Freddie always takes care of his ... "

"Yes, we know, Paul." My mother's tone could have chilled an icebox. "I'll ask him, Dad."

* * * * *

So, thanks to Lieutenant Governor Freddie, Perry began to spend his weekdays at a desk doing clerical work in a state regulatory office near Mac.

One day, a stranger walked through the office door. He approached Perry and asked an odd question. Did he, as a government employee, happen to know anyone who was influential with the governor?

"Why?" Perry asked.

The stranger offered an explanation about a woman who was imprisoned at the Industrial Farm for Women. She would soon be eligible for parole, he said. The Kansas Parole Board had already denied one request for her release. Rumor had it that paying the governor or some other higher-up with clout might get her out quickly. This woman's family was willing to pay handsomely. But it was going to take someone very influential to pull off such a deal.

"Yes," Perry responded. He did know someone who was quite influential.

* * * * *

Though the Browns were willing to fork over a big sum, they were understandably skeptical about doing so without guaranteed results. They had already paid the abortionist's attorneys, Clair Hyter and the late Ed Rooney, a total of $3,600 for parole and clemency. Shortly after Annas Brown had entered prison, her family gave $2,500 to her attorneys. Their understanding was that the money would be returned if she was not released. Some time later, they had handed over an additional $1,100 to Clair Hyter. He was supposed to use it to effect clemency.

121

Neither of their payments had produced anything. Nor was any of the money returned.

Clair Hyter was the only lawyer on her case at this point following the death of Attorney Rooney. Despite his failure to achieve what the family had paid him for, they were willing to retain him. But they wanted to augment his efforts with a powerful legal partner who could spring her from prison as soon as possible. Somehow the Browns had amassed sufficient funds to pay far more than what they had already expended. They hoped that their quantities of cash would get a governor's attention.

My father was maintaining his usual delirious pace by juggling a law practice in Mac with campaigning to get Freddie elected in Topeka. He flitted from place to place and settled once in awhile on Walnut Street, where his presence had become a novelty. In one of these two locales, the Brown family managed to track him down to ask their question.

It was: Would he agree to represent abortionist Annas Brown in her quest for a parole?

Whether he hesitated or not before deciding is impossible to know. But the Browns got the answer they desired.

"Yes," he told them. He would represent Annas Brown.

CHAPTER SEVEN

AN APRIL FOOLS' DAY BRIBE
1955

As my father had promised all along, he was moving us closer to residing in his coveted world of black limousines and gubernatorial splendor. So golden was his political promise that he was alternately gloating and grandiose. All of his campaign efforts had succeeded. The "LET'S CLEAN UP TOPEKA ... " publicity, nights in his Town House apartment, days spent wheedling funds, hours consumed shaking hands, and weeks plotting schemes to acquire more votes had borne victory.

Frederick Lee Hall, 39 years old, had defeated George Docking by a sizable margin. He had become the youngest Kansas governor elected since 1873.

The first reward for a job well done was an invitation from Freddie to speak at his January inauguration. My mother shocked him by agreeing to accompany my father on this auspicious outing. She summoned Grandma Ida to tend us once again.

* * * * *

As my parents prepared to depart for Topeka and Freddie's historic occasion, my sisters and I gathered to participate in the usual fussy farewell. After my father had finally broken free of us to head for the garage, we followed him as far as the back porch. Then we stood waving and yelling goodbye as the Cadillac cruised backward down our driveway.

After the car rounded the bend at our corner and vanished, I stood wondering whether we would be waving at our disappearing parents from the Capitol steps one day very soon. My father always described the state Capitol, on which construction had begun in 1873, as the most beautiful building he had ever seen. He was somber and reverent saying it and offered none of the usual flip mannerisms with which he depicted most everything else. Of course, the imposing statue of Abe Lincoln that graced the sprawling grounds was always the central part of his lavish description.

It seemed to me that it must be wonderful to have a powerful and loyal pal like the new governor. We had heard so much about Freddie for so very long that it felt as if he were a member of our family. He might as well be our important uncle who was moving to a grandiose house and possessed the ability to bestow favors. He had tossed a big one my father's way by asking him to speak at his inaugural. It was another signal that his flashy successor finally stood in the gubernatorial wings.

The imminence of his political dream being realized had started to nag at me. Until lately, the possibility of his becoming governor had loomed far in the future. It had always consisted of a distant mirage toward which we kept traveling. But the people in Mac had begun talking openly about the likelihood of his following Governor Hall into office. They wanted his dream to materialize. So did I. But they would not have to sacrifice life as they knew it like we would.

Who of my friends, I wondered, would want to visit me in the governor's mansion? If they did, where would we fit into a formal building that could accommodate hundreds? I could not imagine us wandering in and out the front door, popping corn in the kitchen, hanging out in the basement, banging on the piano in my bedroom, or practicing cheerleader routines in the front yard as we did in Mac. Would they still like me for who I really was or mostly because my father had become governor?

He would probably become even more of a shadowy figure in our family. He would never have time to lean on the Capitol refrigerator and bestow his morning sunshine. We would no doubt have to spend every single night hidden away upstairs from important guests, absolutely forbidden to appear. What kind of life would that be? Considering it made me ache deep inside.

* * * * *

The next day, we clustered around the kitchen radio to hear my father's speech at the inaugural. Margo, who was somewhat less rowdy than the last time we had gathered for his airwaves address from Hutch, joined us reluctantly. Almost 10 now but still a tomboy, she informed Grandma Ida that she would much prefer some other activity than passively listening to the radio. My dirty look her direction caused Margo to stick out her tongue. Just then, Grandma Ida turned up the radio volume.

"MIII FELLL-OH REEE-PUB-LICK–UNS ... " Suddenly, he was there in our kitchen, but not really.

"SHHH," Grandma Ida said. "Your father is starting."

His voice was confident with a slight waver just as he had practiced in the bathroom. Margo looked my way and careened her eyes as if to say, "We've heard all this before. Do we have to again?"

Quickly, he began issuing platitudes about Freddie. Of course, he did not refer to him so. He substituted lofty preambles such as "Our Honorable" or "The Newly Elected."

I wished that I was clairvoyant and could see Freddie, Leadell, Dad, and Mom up in front of all those people. She was wearing a special suit purchased at Pegues for the occasion. It was grey wool with fur edged about the lapels. She had modeled it for us in her bedroom while testing different shoes and earrings as options. I could imagine her standing there looking beautiful. I wondered what Leadell had chosen for the most important day of her husband's life.

Finally, we heard Freddie's familiar voice whose strains had once drifted out of our dining room. His image marched into our kitchen and

125

stood beside the radio where he talked. I could envision his short frame and those thick spectacles. He was probably gesturing to the crowd who we heard clapping from time to time. My father so admired this man that it was not possible to anticipate that historical accounts would later describe him as "pugnacious, strong, aggressive, fiercely independent, and ambitious." He would also be accused of creating feuds within his supposedly beloved Republican party.

Over the airwaves, the new governor talked about being "put in power by the people" and having "the solemn obligation of service to the people but to administer the affairs of government with efficiency and integrity."

"I describe myself neither as a 'do-gooder' nor a 'do-nothing,'" he went on. "For lack of a better term, I describe myself as a 'do-something.' Perhaps I am what the President has termed a 'progressive moderate.'"

"What's a 'do-something?'" Margo asked.

"SHHH," Grandma Ida whispered as applause drowned out his voice.

Afterward, we were eating tuna fish sandwiches at the kitchen counter when the phone rang. Margo had already performed one of her usual stunts and smeared mayonnaise on her clean shirt. She was no doubt thankful that our mother was not on hand to yell or banish her to the bedroom to contemplate misbehavior. I shushed Margo's apologies and tried to overhear the phone conversation.

"WHAT?" I asked Grandma Ida as soon as she hung up.

Something very important had happened to our father, she said. My first thought was that we would have to move to Topeka right away. Or maybe he would leave us permanently to live there all alone.

Governor Hall had just announced his selection as legal counsel for the Kansas Corporation Commission, she said.

"What's that?" Margo asked.

"I don't know exactly."

"Can I be excused now?" Margo held up her hand.

"Me, too," said Andrea.

"Did you hear what I said about your father's new honor?"

"We want to go play." Margo scooted her chair away from the counter.

Before long, we would learn that this new role as a gubernatorial appointee was to accelerate his pace as a whirling dervish. My memory sees him racing into our kitchen or dining room while issuing a non-stop stream of stories about politics. All of them involved names none of us recognized. He was living most of the time in a world populated by people we did not know and doing things to which we could not relate.

It felt as if he dropped by periodically just to remind us that someone famous headed our household. Then he disappeared again, probably to work at getting more well-known. Or so my sisters and I assumed.

* * * * *

Act One of the mandatory Sunday appearance on Marlin Street had barely commenced when my father made one of his announcements.

"Dad, remember the stranger you told me about who asked if you knew someone influential with the governor? You know, the case of that gal in prison for abortion?" He looked at Perry, who nodded. "Well, they convinced me to represent her." He hesitated as if one of us should say something complimentary.

"What woman?"

"Mrs. Tusswagon, I do believe I told you about her when she was on trial. Annas Brown. The one from Hutch. You're playing Mrs. Sherlock Holmes again."

"What does she look like?"

He issued a vibrating laugh. It was the kind preceding a description of something undesirable. She probably should have been born a man, he said.

127

"A man?" I remembered him reading to me that the newspaper had called her portly and stout. They had never described her as looking like a guy.

She was tough, short, wide, crude, and masculine, he said.

"Do you have a picture of her?"

"No." He said the only newspaper photo he had seen of her was at the time of the murder. She had looked menacing. Maybe the papers had feared that printing more pictures of her would scare their readers. He chortled.

Without snapshots or verbal word pictures to lead me, I sat in Hattie's kitchen and invented my own version of his first meeting with his client at the prison. The dull sheen of his silk suit glimmered beneath dull lights in the depressing room. He carried his black briefcase in one hand. The other, usually clenching a cigarette, swung freely since smoking was probably verboten there. He glanced about and could hardly suppress his curiosity about other inmates who sat behind glass partitions with small openings. They, like Annas Brown, had to talk with visitors through those smudged circles.

I wondered whether he had smiled or looked somber as he sat facing the abortionist's harsh countenance. Had he winced at the sight of her homely face? "Older than the mother of God," he had probably thought. But he must have reminded himself that his mission was to obtain her confidence in him and not to criticize her appearance. Tough as she was, he would have to handle her carefully. His murderous client seemed unafraid of anything or anyone.

It would not gel in my mind until much later that Annas Brown, like Freddie, had been hovering around the fringes of our family for awhile by then. My father had mentioned the abortionist's name once in awhile, usually in reference to some other controversial legal issue. "Like that Brown law case," he would say. "Makes me think of that Mrs. Brown," he had said once after a sleazy individual sought his legal assistance. Disgust had never infiltrated his voice in reference to her. He had not said, "Can you imagine doing something so awful?" or "Taking the life of an unborn child is terribly wrong."

After Gracie described abortion as slaughtering babies, Annas Brown had taken up permanent residence in a dark corner of my mind. Black fantasies of a shadowy woman carrying a dagger or a long pair of scissors had started to appear when I thought of her. With her weapon held high, she had moved stealthily toward the swollen belly of a woman who was lying on her back. The impending horror had frozen there, but sometimes not before I heard an imaginary scream or the cackle of a witch.

Before Mrs. Brown had come along, my father represented run-of-the-mill legal clients. Mennonites traveled in horse-drawn buggies from their farms, outside Mac, to his office for help. Disgruntled property owners showed up to file actions against foes. People buying or selling houses sought his legal expertise. He dabbled in various small arenas of the law.

His most favored legal pastime was title work. He liked playing detective and researching who owned titles to certain properties. It caused him to travel to the gas-producing areas of Kansas, and the oil fields of neighboring Oklahoma, to ascertain land ownership. He relished glad-handing wildcatters out in those dusty fields and slipping them snippets of political wisdom.

He had never represented a murderess. After all, Mac was not the sort of town where such scandalous happenings took place.

My mother must have gagged at the thought of Annas Brown's evil practices. She and her friends, that tight clique who sewed and played bridge in weekly clubs, revered motherhood. It had replaced the careers for which college educated them. Instead of excelling as experts in office or school settings, they had chosen to specialize in creating casseroles and stitching seams. And rearing perfect children.

Not one of them would have considered destroying a fetus, whether it was wanted or not. "Caboose" or "our little surprise" they would say

129

of a baby born five or six years after their last child had entered kindergarten. Once a doctor had confirmed their suspicions about missed periods, they would dutifully haul out the stored diapers and maternity smocks or borrow them from friends.

I have no recollection of my parents discussing Annas Brown or even abortion. But then they always dealt with such matters behind closed doors where children could not ascertain clues about life in the world of adults.

* * * * *

Traditionally, April Fools' Day pitted me against my father. Or vice versa. It offered a delicious annual opportunity to return some of the nonsense he doled out daily. Pouring salt in his morning coffee ranked as my favorite prank. A dash of soy sauce was my second choice.

"Ye Gods, Mrs. Tusswagon!" he usually yelped after a sip.

"April Fools'!" I shouted.

He sabotaged me later in the day by slipping Tabasco or garlic salt into my milk. Or he phoned from his office to bellow in a disguised voice, "April Fools'!" Then he hung up as if I would never guess who it was.

His absence this particular April Fools' Day made me miss our silly rituals. Surely he would phone from his Topeka apartment, I thought. But he did not. Probably he was too busy with something political, I finally decided after dinner.

There was no reason to suspect that my father was absent and did not play jokes because he was occupied conducting a fateful April Fools' Day meeting in his Town House apartment. He had invited a small group of guests there for a significant purpose. They had traveled by train from Hutch to Topeka, where he picked them up at Union Station. His intent was to plot the parole of Annas Brown.

Hutch attorney Clair Hyter, who co-represented her, was on hand.

So was her former husband John Brown and their daughter Lucille Updegraffe. A mystery guest would join them after my father telephoned him at the State Capitol. He was a youthful fellow with the unwieldy name of Starling Mack Nations. Most everyone called him Mack. He was a newspaperman by profession, and was now working as executive secretary to Governor Hall.

There was no way for me to know either on this April Fools' that my father had already consulted Freddie, more than once, about the Annas Brown parole. When Freddie had visited Mac the year before, during a campaign stop, my father broached the parole matter with him.

"Hall told me not to take any action until he was elected as he would have his own Pardon Attorney," my father would later testify.

The month before his April Fools' meeting, he had spoken again with Hall about the possibility of parole. There had been a certain urgency about resolving the matter as the Kansas Parole Board was scheduled to meet on April 6th. Their agenda would include a request for an early release of the abortionist.

With his guests gathered about him in the motel apartment, my father informed them that he had determined an appropriate sum for the Browns to pay for a parole.

"Twenty-five thousand dollars," he said.

Later, he would testify that Mack Nations had suggested the sum which stunned his small audience, and would amount to about $188,000 today. He would also maintain that in a prior conversation about a parole, Nations had told him that "he would be glad to cooperate in any way he could."

The Browns' reaction to a $25,000 bailout was not encouraging. "They hit the ceiling – said it was more than she could pay – that she didn't have that kind of money," my father would recall.

Though he made no mention of fee dispersal, he would make it clear later on that he should get $5,000. Governor Hall and Mack Nations would receive $10,000 each. In case the IRS somehow learned about this cash dispersal, he had devised a strategy for that, too. The governor and his secretary could categorize their money "not as a fee but as a political contribution."

During his meeting, my father summoned Mack Nations by phone to come to the Town House. He arrived in about 15 minutes, and would later paint a comedic picture of events following the $25,000 bombshell announcement.

"There was a huddle in the bathroom with Hyter and the woman, and maybe Lackie, and they came out and said they didn't think they could get more than $10,000. Lackie asked me to talk to the governor about it and I said I would. He asked me to call him back, and again, I said I would."

The governor's executive secretary followed through on his assignment. After conferring with his boss, he telephoned the Town House to say that "it could be arranged."

But the payoff planners needed the abortionist's approval, and access to her money. So Clair Hyter, Lucille Updegraffe and John Brown left Topeka and were chauffeured in my father's car to the Lansing prison. They planned to ask her for $15,000 — $10,000 for the parole and $5,000 for a possible pardon.

Although my father was ostensibly the lead attorney, it was Clair Hyter who headed into the prison to seek the abortionist's cooperation. Lucille accompanied him. They left John Brown and my father behind in the car to wait.

About four years later, my father would swear in testimony before the IRS that his abortionist client could easily afford a $25,000 parole. He would claim that Mack Nations had been his source for such information about her wealth because his mother was employed at the Industrial Farm and knew Annas Brown.

* * * * *

On April 6th, as the Parole Board met to consider Annas Brown's petition for an early release, the bribe plotters were lunching in Kansas City. Afterward, my father, Clair Hyter, John Brown and his daughter, Lucille, went to the Hotel New Yorker. There my father made repeated phone calls to ascertain whether Annas Brown would be freed. Not until late afternoon did he learn that his client's request had been denied. She would be eligible to reapply in April 1956.

Though my father would later claim that he left the Brown case as of April 6th, the parole bid was not to be abandoned. Behind-the-scenes negotiations continued.

In early August, when the Parole Board met again, Annas Brown's request for release was inexplicably on the agenda. This time, the Board granted her wish. She would be released on August 20th with one stipulation: Annas Brown had to reside in a state other than Kansas for the first two years of her parole. She would choose Etowah, Tennessee, where her niece lived.

Neither my father nor the abortionist had any way of knowing it, but they resembled a pair of errant constellations careening toward each other on an irreversible course. They were destined for a catastrophic collision. Those hard-working gods of fate had deigned to interrelate their lives at a far more profound level than simply that of attorney and client. One of them would survive the inevitable debacle. The other would not.

* * * * *

On Saturday morning, August 20th, the drama of Parole Day began to unfold. It was a production with scenes in two diverse geographical settings. The cast consisted of seven major players, two invisible actors, and a pair of bit participants.

It was no doubt a typically steamy late summer morning all about Wyandotte County. Heat probably hovered over front doors of the

Lansing prison since it was located at the bottom of a deep bowl-shape space as if to hide it from area residents.

At mid-morning, Attorney Hyter arrived there from his home in Hutch. He wore a business suit and tie, which must have been stifling. Somehow he had been selected as the point man to finalize the parole and its payoff. For this momentous occasion, he had chosen to drive a car belonging to John Brown. His only passenger was Annas Brown's daughter, Lucille.

Earlier that morning, the abortionist had been advised abruptly of her imminent freedom. At least she would so claim later, when describing her summons to the prison office for the exhilarating news. She was to be freed after serving just three years and eight months of her five-to-21-year sentence.

Once inside, Attorney Hyter finalized the release arrangements. Then he escorted the abortionist and Lucille out to the parking lot. They headed toward Highway 40 outside Lansing and a specific service station.

Another Brown family car, and its occupants, waited there. Annas Brown's other daughter, her former husband, a niece and her husband formed the welcoming committee.

Understandably, the Brown clan was in the mood to celebrate. But first, they needed to hand over their thick stack of $100 bills. John Brown was the designated money man. Once he had produced the weighty bundle of bills, the murderess counted them out for Clair Hyter, who sat with a briefcase propped on his lap. He tallied the cash again until satisfied that it totaled $10,000. Then he tucked the bills into his briefcase. That accomplished, he waited for the rest of his money. He had asked the Browns to supply an additional $1,750 in the form of travelers checks. That was to pay for what he had identified as legal services. After that had been delivered, the attorney stuffed the checks into his coat pocket.

Business transactions completed, one of the Brown contingent expressed the hankering for a soft drink. So the paroled prisoner and her joyous family trooped into the service station restaurant with their nervous attorney. He refused to join them for liquid refreshment. He would not even sit down with them. Instead, he paced the restaurant aisle and muttered periodically that he must be in Topeka by two o'clock to meet the governor.

* * * * *

Clair Hyter encountered eerie silence as he entered the spacious halls of the state Capitol in downtown Topeka that Saturday afternoon. No one strolled the corridors or called out greetings. This total lack of activity was an inherent part of the plot so as to ensure secrecy. But at least one person was somewhere in the building. He was awaiting a two o'clock rendezvous on the second floor in an office that belonged to the executive secretary of Governor Hall.

Attorney Hyter, in his state of anxiety, had arrived an hour ahead of schedule. But he mounted a regal winding staircase to the second floor anyway. There he entered the office and met Mack Nations. He did not seem surprised that the governor's executive secretary was there instead of the governor. He was told that Fred Hall had left town 24 hours before. The governor planned to deliver a Kansas Day picnic speech in Manitou Springs, Colorado, and would be away for nearly a week.

So the governor's executive secretary and the Brown attorney began to conduct business. Having no witnesses but each other, they somehow managed to concoct completely contradictory accounts of their meeting.

Later, both did agree that Clair Hyter handed Mack Nations a sealed envelope bulging with the $10,000 in cash. They also concurred that the attorney asked for $200 to cover additional legal expenses. The similarity of their stories ended there.

The Clair Hyter version was that Mack Nations responded to his request by opening the envelope and handing him $200.

135

The Mack Nations rendition was that he never opened the envelope and locked it in a special drawer of his desk. He intended to give it to the governor later.

The only major player in this August 20th drama whose whereabouts were unknown was Annas Brown's other attorney, Paul Lackie. He was fully aware of the play's scenario and timetable, of course, since he had plotted it. But he had cleverly managed to extricate himself entirely from mechanics of the actual payoff.

CHAPTER EIGHT

DESCENT INTO HELL
1956-1958

"I have an announcement to make," my father said, striving for his most arresting political timbre.

He had summoned us to the Walnut Street kitchen on a Saturday morning for an unusual family summit. We had become accustomed to his political pronouncements in this room. After years of them, we were nearly numb. Their frequency caused me to look at him every once in awhile and nod during his delivery to feign interest.

Dining room dinners had been the usual setting for his most significant political bulletins. There, over pork chops and mashed potatoes, we had learned of his Young GOP candidacy. There, consuming ham and lima beans, we had heard about his decision to represent Annas Brown. Maybe he always selected our regal dining room for startling political news because the kitchen was not sufficiently dramatic. That being my theory, I assumed that this announcement was to be something minor.

He appeared before us that May morning of 1956 in a short-sleeved shirt and nondescript dark pants instead of a handsome suit and lush tie. It made him appear devoid of a destination. He held a cigarette in a hand that seemed to tremble without pause.

"I want to tell you ... " he started before clearing his throat. His eyes swept past my mother, who sat examining her nails, and around my sisters and me. He appeared reluctant to continue. Finally, he blurted, "We are moving."

"To a new house?" Margo asked.

"No." His tone was curt. "No, to another town. Independence, Kansas." He rushed to add that famous people like playwright William

Inge had grown up in this fine town. He began rambling about the fact that I had recently appeared as an extra in the river bank scenes of the Picnic movie, based on Inge's play, that were filmed near Hutch. He knew that the thrill of it had made me consider myself somewhat of a candidate for Hollywood stardom. So his eyes beseeched me as if this bit of trivia could ease the traumatic news he had just delivered.

"I don't want to move." Margo broke into sobs.

"I don't either." A tear trickled down Andrea's cheek.

"Knock it off," he said, frowning at them. "Someday you'll have a life of your own but this one is mine."

Confronted with our distraught faces, he backtracked to offer a sunny version of his bombshell. This Independence experience would be fabulous, he predicted. Think of the new friends we were bound to make. And wait until we met the Independence pal who had convinced him to relocate, that Republican bigwig, Walter Wilson. Remember the fellow he always called "Walter-Never-Falter-Wilson," who had supported his GOP candidacy? This man was a real mover. He was going to be a terrific asset in his race to be governor, he said.

The Senator had been a "right fine" law partner, he said. Don't misunderstand that. His name still impressed the older Republican crowd. But he was getting up there into the old codger category and losing his clout with younger politicians, who were running the party. This Walter-Never-Falter was a GOP up-and-comer though. He was considerably younger, had plenty of name recognition, and was a real good ole boy.

At that moment, I was flooded with dislike for my father. My 16-year-old mind suggested that he had no right to jerk all of us around for the sake of his political advancement. It was cruel of him to force us to abandon the only life we had known. He was about to snatch us from our comfortable cocoon of Mac to live in some strange town just because one of his Republican pals had made promises.

I looked at Andrea, who had tears streaking her cheeks, and Margo whose pouting expression was in overdrive.

I watched my mother inhale a cigarette deeply as she retreated into that inner world where we could not follow. I thought about how all those days and nights of her pleading, demanding, and cajoling my father to abandon politics had once struck me as selfish. I had wondered then why she objected to his being famous. Why had she not wanted to display her considerable domestic talents in a governor's mansion? Why had she not wanted him to be happy?

Now his ambitions had brought us here, with my sisters in tears and my mother crushed as if a bulldozer had run her over.

More than ever, I yearned for a normal dad who did not mimic a whirling cyclone, lived with his family, did not drink until he wove, and never engaged in pink apartment dalliances. Most of all, I longed for him to be vibrant and irreverent again.

His personality transformation from sunny to sullen had been evolving slowly, like a silken spider web spun strand by strand. It had been so gradual that, until this jarring relocation pronouncement, I had not focused on it. But his "Someday you'll have a life … " jab at my sisters struck me as alien rhetoric from someone who could not tolerate hurt feelings. His upbeat verbal outpourings, which used to assault us daily, had trickled down slowly to mundane and vague laments about this or that. He was testy, too, with a level of crankiness that robbed him of charm and sometimes made him surly.

He had never offered us the specifics of events like Freddie's failure to seek his campaign management services in the bid for a second gubernatorial term. He had hardly acknowledged it at all. Neither had we heard details about his abrupt dismissal as legal counsel for the Kansas Corporation Commission. When that had occurred he said so little that it hardly seemed momentous.

Later, I would realize that these two seminal events might have been overshadowed by his exultation at the prison release of Annas Brown. It was a coup and all his own doing, he had advised us. That Hyter lawyer from Hutch had never been able to spring her, he bragged.

The feat had required the services of one P.A.L., Tall Paul, Peck's Bad Boy, chairman of the Young GOP, the elated victor who stood right there before us in the personage of our father.

None of us had thought to ask why he felt that an abortionist, whose illegal vocation was destroying unborn lives, had been someone worth championing. We had also failed to address obvious moral questions concerning his exuberance at turning her loose to do more of the same. But in the Annas Brown days, my father had still been the euphoric politician who could persuade you that a green object was actually blue if examined in the proper light.

* * * * *

The night before our moving van arrived, I heard my mother creeping through the rooms of her beloved house to tell it goodbye. Her footsteps creaked on the landing of our front stair steps and moved past the stained glass window, which shed daytime light patterns like a prism. She had already toured the dining room with its dramatic gold medallion wallpaper and white shell-motif cupboards that stored her silver tea service, the kitchen where a plumber had fallen through the floor opening into the basement during a remodeling project, and the living room where our bewitching Christmas tree had soared to the ceiling for more than a decade.

Not once had she spoken to my sisters and me about our imminent uprooting. But the look in her eyes told me that her heart was fractured.

I had learned recently that she had harbored a dreadful secret during 15 of my 16 years. It had helped me begin to understand the dark agony that sometimes engulfed her face. Maybe she had no intention of ever divulging the tragedy until being forced to during my questions about family genealogy.

She had willingly furnished background information about various relatives such as her grandparents, who immigrated from Sweden

140

and Germany to farm and mill wheat from the thriving Kansas fields. She had offered descriptions of Grandma Ida's repressive parents, who considered sewing or dancing verboten on Sundays, and Grandpa Emil's flamboyant father and aristocratic mother. Then my questions had turned to her own father, who died eight days preceding my first birthday.

"Tell me about Grandpa Emil" had made her dissolve instantly into heaving sobs. Tears careened down her cheeks, making her seem like a child who was being punished.

"He killed himself." She had choked on the words as if bile were flooding her throat. Between jagged crying intervals, she had blurted scanty details. His paralyzing stroke. A life sentence for a vigorous man of being bedridden. The shotgun that had fired on the night of May Day, 1940. Grandma Ida becoming an instant widow in her 50s. She did not need to add that no family member had ever mentioned it since.

Finished with her blurted secret, she had flashed one of her "That's enough" looks.

* * * * *

My mother was wearing the identical expression as we headed across Mac to Marlin Street for our final Sunday matinee. My father offered no DO NOT lecture en route other than a stern warning not to upset Hattie more than she already was. He was jittery. Perspiration coated his brow and his tremulous hands fiddled with the steering wheel.

My sisters and I were uncharacteristically mute. We failed to offer our usual complaint: "Why do we have to go to Hattie and Perry's every Sunday? It's so boring." We knew that these tedious Sabbath homages were about to become a bittersweet memory. We would no longer sniff the scent of cinnamon rolls and cherry pie, or be asked if we wanted a chocolate-covered cherry. There would be no more trooping past the pink telephone or surreptitious counting of figurines behind glass cabinet doors.

141

Something seemed so wrong about all of this. I felt like we were about to depart on a trip but no one could tell us exactly why we were going, or what direction we were headed. And I could not help but wonder where Josie fit into it all.

As we stood outdoors on the Marlin Street driveway and watched the requisite lifting of the window shade, I waited for my father's "Easier to get into Fort Knox than my own damned house." But it did not come.

In the kitchen, Hattie sat on her stool in a position resembling a fetus, arms wrapped around her frail chest. She rocked slightly, side to side, and did not glance up as my father approached.

"We're not leaving for Timbuktu, for God's Sake." He attempted a partial smile, and issued some lame suggestion about becoming Kansas governor. "Mama, please." He patted her shoulder.

Watching their intimate tableau, I wondered how he could bear to part from her. It was not the first time it had occurred to me that it must be a glorious feeling to be considered absolutely perfect by your mother, as my father did. I had fantasized before about how it would feel to bask in constant endearments such as "Dearest Paul Andrew" and "My Darling Treasure," and have a mother's papery lips move across the back of your neck. I had decided that such reassurances of perfection, like Hattie bestowed, would surely beat at your heart like a lifelong lullaby. They would cause you to soar and swoop as unconditional love could.

After what seemed an eternity, she substituted sobbing for dabbing her eyes with a soaked handkerchief. Perry had remained silent throughout and failed to utter, "Why would anybody in their right mind want to live anywhere but Mac?"

"Guess it's time to say goodbye," my father said. "Well, not goodbye. Rather ... " He stumbled over the words, trying to back out of it.

Hattie rose at his cue. She wobbled a bit before heading upstairs to retrieve her Wheat Money.

* * * * *

The next morning, a big truck pulled up at the Walnut Street curb to change our lives. The Senator walked across the street to say farewell and wish us good luck. As we stood talking, there was no way to know that this departure would be the start of an eight-year odyssey. It would involve four inexplicable moves and wrenching emotions. There was no crystal ball to advise us that each of these abrupt relocations would cause my skin to prickle with a sense that we were being chased by invisible demons.

We followed the truck to Independence, and then wound through unfamiliar streets to the house my father had rented for us. We peered at a structure that sat at the end of a ridiculously long sidewalk. A screened porch stretched across the front. Two tall frame stories seemed to tilt precariously to the left.

We approached the front door as gingerly as if a misstep could destroy us all. Inside, the living room floor sloped sufficiently that a coin would roll down it. "Like being on a listing ship," joked our Navy officer to his vacant-eyed wife. It was my mother's first sight of her new abode. Her glances portended doom. Nothing about this substitute for her stately Walnut Street showplace made her eyes glimmer. The square ordinary rooms and dark cramped kitchen seemed devoid of possibilities. There were none of the charming nooks and crannies we had known. The yard had no hollyhocks alongside the garage or splen-did cherry tree in the back yard.

"Not quite as grand as Walnut, I realize. Or the governor's manse," he said. "But we'll find another one to buy soon."

We may have abandoned Mac. But we had brought along our best political faces to wear before a new community of voters. We practiced donning them after a photographer telephoned from the local newspa-per. He wanted to visit and snap our portrait as the new Independence family headed by a potential governor.

My mother, who interpreted the honor as a photo shoot for the entire house, tore about arranging furniture and hanging pictures. Her efforts proved fruitless. All he wanted to record on film were my father, mother, and The Harem seated perfectly packaged on our striped sofa. He suggested that Spot would add a warm and homey touch. So our shivering Dalmatian joined us at Margo's feet to address the camera with eyes of two different colors.

On the day of the photo's publication, my father purchased stacks of newspapers. "This family sh-oooore knows how to pose," he said, holding up the newsprint of our photo. "We'd be a mighty fine-looking first family in the governor's manse."

Walter-Never-Falter-Wilson came to call with his wife one evening. He filled our living room with bluster. "Welcome to Indy," he boomed in a baritone voice. His fleshy face bore small red vein marks, and his nose looked bulbous. He gyrated with a drink in one hand and carried on about my father, who would soon become the first governor to hail from Indy. Why, this was already the home town breeding ground of another celebrity, he said. His name was William Inge. "Billy, we call him."

I studied Walter-Never-Falter and did not understand. Why would my father want to fraternize with a politician who evoked a Teddy Roosevelt caricature? It was difficult not to compare this political blowhard to The Senator, who had resembled Cary Grant. Something told me that we had shifted castes, down a notch, by coming to this strange town for reasons none of us understood.

But Indy did prove to be a friendly spot, just as Walter-Never-Falter had described it. Neighbors arrived with plates of cookies. A local version of Welcome Wagon phoned to set an appointment. My father haunted the VFW and pronounced it passable, though certainly not up to Mac standards.

Margo, Andrea and I were devoid of acquaintances to serve as summer companions. So we turned to one another. We baked chocolate chip

144

cookies, cranked up the radio volume, and sang along with the Beatles in our minuscule kitchen. It caused us to argue about one sister eating too much cookie dough or another spilling flour on the floor. When I told them to do the dishes, they returned the inevitable dirty looks. One by one, we marked summer days off the calendar until school was to start. We never suspected that our newfound camaraderie was lashing us together like seamen about to set sail on turbulent waters.

Just as in Mac, my father was forever on his way out of town. Sometimes Marlin Street in Mac was the destination. He dashed off in response to the urgency of a Hattie Spell or his own deficit of cash. By now, her hysterical entreaties to him were so embedded in the fabric of our family that we regarded her daily phone calls as routine. My sisters and I had committed to memory the irritated countenance of our mother as the animated voice of our father conducted his side of the phone conversation. It followed a predictable course.

"Yes, Mama. How are you feeling, Mama? Oh, rather poorly? Now, now, you're not going to leave us for the beyond right away. Yes, I can come. No, not right this minute. A Spell? Yes, I'll be there as soon as I can."

"Hattie is fine, Paul," my mother usually said in one of her weary pronouncements about her mother-in-law. It was unreasonable for him to react to another of her false alarms.

"Mama sounded sick on the phone" or "She just had a Spell," he would counter. After all, her heart was so weak from that rheumatic fever. What if something happened to her and he failed to be there? As my sisters and I listened, our heads bobbed back and forth between them like apples floating in a Halloween water tub.

It seemed to me that the specter of my grandmother had filled every house we ever occupied. No matter where we lived, she continued to hover over us and haunt our rooms. She was an apparition forever sad about a trifling slight by my mother, angry about a statement made that none of us could remember, or certain that an impending malady would soon take her into the beyond.

When my father's destination was not Mac, there were urgent political matters that needed tending in Topeka. "Ye Gods, this is an election year," he reminded us with appropriately dramatic gestures.

Our schools proved as welcoming as the new neighbors. Slowly, the agony of leaving Mac abated. Margo and Andrea began to bring friends home after school to play. My mother took up bridge and baked lasagna again. And I landed a beefy football captain boyfriend, who escorted me as a member of the homecoming court. The Harem seemed to be fathered by an increasingly important celebrity, too. Remarks like "I saw your dad's picture in the paper" or "You're the daughter of that politician" only made us feel more accepted.

* * * * *

The thunderbolt announcement that Freddie had been defeated in the Republican primary by Warren W. Shaw resides in my memory bank, for whatever reason, as a defining moment. My father announced it by phone from Topeka, leaving Mom to deliver the news.

Freddie's defeat for reelection to a second gubernatorial term shocked us because my father had insisted all along that he was a shoo-in. Evidently, he had assumed that voters would forgive the constant conflicts that had characterized Freddie's first term. He had theorized that they would ignore his questionable tactics like firing the State Purchasing Agency director, and then changing membership of the State Civil Service Commission before he could appeal his dismissal. He had supposed that voters would not hold the biggest controversy of his tenure against him either. That had occurred when he vetoed the "Right to Work" bill. The legislation, approved by both houses of the Kansas legislature, would have eliminated the requirement that laborers join a union when employed in unionized shops and factories.

Now Freddie was about to become a has-been governor. The shocking situation caused a thick layer of gloom to begin spreading through the rooms of our Independence rental. The resulting change in my father seemed to accelerate the decline in his positivism, which had begun shortly before leaving Mac. He camouflaged his level of disappointment by predicting that Republicans would no doubt want Freddie as their candidate in the next election.

"What the hell is wrong with Kansas voters anyway?" he moaned.

Yet we no longer heard him sing at all behind his bathroom door. He seemed intolerant of innocuous events and more restless than ever. He cursed the body that had always been his prized gem and dabbed at bloody razor cuts on his face with shaking hands. "Damnation. Can't even hold a razor steady," he said. Coffee slapped side to side in his cup as vibrating hands failed him there, too. Even his memory, the "steel trap" he had always described, was acting up. He might leave a room and then return panicky, sure of having forgotten a cigarette burning. Or he missed law appointments at his office and blamed the errors on his secretary.

Walter-Never-Falter was his biggest complaint. He bemoaned the unfulfilled promises he had made to lure him to Indy, and frequent disagreements on strategies to get him elected governor. He didn't even use his partner's nickname anymore, referring to him as "that damned Wilson."

* * * * *

On election day in November, a political hatchet fell on the Republicans. Democratic challenger George Docking, or "Duuuh Docking" as my father had dubbed him, became governor-elect of a state that nearly always elected Republicans.

"Damn it. Kansans ALWAYS vote Republican," he exploded. "Sunflower State people should know better than to elect a dumb Democrat." Besides, Abilene's own Dwight Eisenhower was running the entire country. Wouldn't they want their governor to be from the same party? Well, they would choose a Republican next time, he predicted. Maybe not even Freddie.

"Maybe ... " He waited for one of us to say, "Maybe you, Dad?"

He began to return from each Topeka trip more dejected than the one before. Democrats were throwing their new power around even though Duuuh Docking had yet to be sworn in, he complained. His good ole Republican cronies, who had once been fixtures at his beloved Pickles bar, were starting to vanish. All that the damned Topeka newspaper wrote about now was "Docking this" and "Docking that," he said. Even his favorite Topeka restaurant, where he had devoured multiple servings of coconut cream pie with ice cream, seemed different.

The air surrounding my father, once airy like spun cotton candy, had become as heavy as the atmospheric pressure preceding a Kansas hailstorm.

* * * * *

Thanksgiving was nearly at hand when he convened another family meeting in the dining room. He sat at the table to address us. His eyes churned. One of his legs jiggled violently as if trying to match the rhythm of African drumbeats. It was the predictable signal that duress was nipping at his core. His foot vibrated on the sloping wood floor below my mother's walnut table. But he failed to offer the usual "listing ship" joke.

"Things haven't worked out quite like I hoped here in Indy," he said tentatively, rotating his eyes. "Goes to show you that old saying about not being able to tell a book by its cover. Damned Wilson. Anyway, politics ... "

It made me tune out his instant rationalizations about why life in Kansas had suddenly become intolerable with a Democrat at the helm and Missouri might be a better place to test new Republican political waters.

"We're moving" is all I heard.

The dining room was so still that I could hear my heart thumping. Margo, Andrea and I glared at him. We rejected his horrendous words before drifting off into our private arenas of grief. He was ripping our hearts again and tearing out roots we had barely begun planting. All the while, he was babbling about politics as if our priority should still be that he became governor.

Like celluloid strips passing on a movie reel, I saw myself walk onto the Independence High School football field in a herringbone suit, pinned with a corsage, and a homecoming crown tilted on my head. I envisioned myself at other games soaring above ground with a cheer-leading megaphone in one hand. Mostly, I pictured the green-eyed athlete who had stolen the remaining chunk of my heart that had not been left behind in Mac six months before.

I could hear my father saying back then, "Someday you will have a life of your own but this one is mine." He was wrong. I was sure of it. My life mattered, too. And I wanted it to remain the same. I resented him at that moment in a way that felt frightening. What right did he have to decimate the lives of Mom, Margo, Andrea and me all for the sake of his political prize?

The unsettling sensation that we were being chased surfaced one more time. The pursuers were invisible but biting at our heels. Their relentless pursuit of us had completely altered life as we had once known it. Freddie and The Senator, and now Walter-Never-Falter, had been among the casualties. So were we. Yet we had no idea what was causing us to flee.

We were moving to K-Ceee, my father was saying. Our supposedly joyous destination was Kansas City, Missouri, and his new job with a title company. Our house could not be in the Kansas part of the city, a segment of which is divided like a clean knife cut from Missouri by State Line Road. We must live in Mizz-oooh, he said. As usual, there was no explanation. He reeled off superlatives about K-Ceee attrac-

149

tions that Mac and Indy could not possibly offer. Professional baseball games. The Kansas City Royal horse show. Those famous stockyards with their juicy steaks. The Country Club Plaza and its fabulous Christmas lights.

Missouri loomed as a foreign country to my sisters and me. We believed that Kansas featured everything necessary for a bucolic existence. We had been weaned on the sight of her wheat stalks swaying like upright silk beneath cerulean skies. We knew her rhythms as our own. The spring burst of velvet pussy willows. The hushed stillness before a tornado. The summer furnace blast winds. My father had always insisted that the soil was richer and the people friendlier among the sunflowers than in any other state. It had made us feel blessed.

How my mother reacted to the K-Ceee residency news remains blurry in my memory. The forbidding look on her face, or retreats to her inner sanctum, probably got buried in the magnitude of my personal grief. I suppose it was possible that she found the prospect of a city appealing. She could return to being the stylish woman who used to laugh with friends and wore red stilettos. Maybe she thought that my father's political ambitions would diminish once we were located across the state line. That theory would have to mean, though, that she had been ignoring his references to a prominent Kansas Republican making waves in the Democratic stronghold of Mizz-oooh.

* * * * *

My sisters and I approached Kansas City like soldiers being marched away to detention. For me, it turned out to be exactly that.

As we settled into a small Tudor-style stucco house, Mom tried to soft-sell the ominous information that my new school of more than 2,000 students had literary societies. She divulged nothing while driving me past the massive building that could easily have housed the high schools of Mac and Indy under its roof. The prospect of this giant institution generated nightmares.

150

Bob, a kid next door, volunteered to escort me to Southwest High the first day. No advance warnings could have prepared me for the throngs of girls in heavy makeup who wore prominently displayed literary membership pins on cashmere sweaters. As I examined them, they failed to notice me. I might as well have been invisible. That was exactly what I longed to become. Then they would not have been able to see me weeping as I escaped into the frosty world outside and ran as far away as my legs could take me. Just six months ago, I had been the new and popular girl in a different school. Now, I was testing that role again. But no one seemed to comprehend that I was an alien who was deprived of friends, giggles, and weekend parties. I belonged nowhere.

Each day, I slipped through school hallways where no one spoke to me and into classrooms where everybody knew one another. Waves of longing for Indy or Mac washed through my days.

"I hate it here," I howled to Mom daily after school. "None of those snobby girls want more friends. Why did we have to move to this horrible place?"

My father had begun talking openly about Missouri politics as if he could cross into a Democratic state and run for Republican governor with Kansas qualifications. "Lord knows Mizz-oooh could benefit from a different guv," he said to us in the dining room with wood shutters at its windows. "I do know a thing or two about that." He meandered off into some soliloquy about dirty Missouri politics and that Pendergast crowd who had held political sway for years. Maybe they had even manipulated Give-Em-Hell-Harry, he suggested.

Much as I resented what he had done to us, it was oddly reassuring to hear renewed political rambling from a dad who never attended Republican rallies or rushed off for speeches anymore. That person had disappeared, making it eerily quiet in our new house. No Pied Piper marched through to toss campaign slogans and theories our way. No political notables or governors arrived for dinner or even phoned to speak with my father.

His resurrected interest in politics made me hope that the vigor we used to know would return and the funny dad who had seasoned our days with political jargon would come with him. Maybe it would make his sense of desperation vanish. For I could feel that he was slipping away, drawn to Kansas City's lure of anonymous bars where it was easy to hide. He dined with us and talked politics one night. Then he detonated and failed to show up the next.

One school night, quite late, the telephone rang a long time in my parents' upstairs bedroom. My mother had remained steadfast in her refusal to answer it once she was in bed. So I raced out of my room and down the dark hall.

A bartender introduced himself on the phone and said he was calling from downtown. He explained that my father, his inebriated patron swaying on a bar stool, had forgotten where his car was parked. It was nearly closing time, but he would wait if someone wanted to pick him up. He offered an address.

"Excuse me." I left the phone to shake my mother awake and explain.

"Let him find his own way home," she said without hesitation.

"Put him in a cab," I told the bartender after giving our address. "Have the driver honk in front of our house if my father doesn't have any money."

I paced the dining room, clutching cash from my mother's purse and watching for approaching headlights on our ink-black street. Finally, the cab pulled up. Peeking through the shutters, I saw a door open and the passenger lurch while handing the driver money. I tore up the front hall steps, rushed into the dark shadows of my room, and slipped between the sheets. I did not want to find out whether he fumbled the front door key, fell against the frame, or cursed his own incompetence.

After such episodes, he was a repentant adult child who sought forgiveness and sympathy from his own children. "I'm sorry. It'll never happen again," he said to us. "Your Mr. Pops do love ya. Yes, I loves ya. Do you love me, too?"

We had been in K-Ceee less than two months when startling news arrived via the Kansas political grapevine. The nature of it made me wonder whether my father had known about it before then. Maybe it explained his seeking ever more refuge in a bottle.

The scandalous bulletin concerned the fact that Freddie, in the waning days of his administration, had committed an act that produced outcries of foul ethics among Kansans. But he was smart enough to know that his move, sometimes called a "triple-jump," was legal.

Shortly before his gubernatorial term was to expire, a Kansas Supreme Court justice had announced his retirement. It prompted Freddie to resign as governor. That cleared the way for the new interim governor, Lieutenant Governor John McCuish, to appoint him to the vacant Supreme Court post. As a result, Freddie was sitting on the Kansas Supreme Court, and my father was salving his political wounds in smoky bars.

As he poured booze down his throat, he must have been thinking that those political gods had muddled the original schema that he and his one-time crony created. It had been intended as a coattail scenario, in which one would lead the other to political Mecca. They had never factored in negative detours, like primary defeats or discarded friendships. A Supreme Court post had never been mentioned at all. From the outset, the two participants in this political diagram had been destined to share the prize 50-50.

* * * * *

My father seemed to notice, occasionally, that I was following him in a downward personal spiral. He tweaked my cheek, looked me over head to feet, and warned me not to turn into a "fat Mrs. Tusswagon."

But I was becoming an addict like him. Only I sought refuge in pans of brownies and cartons of ice cream rather than liquor bottles.

While he was cruising bars late at night, I was committing sin in the kitchen.

"You could be a beauty queen if you lose some weight," Mom said.

"Can I make some chocolate chip cookies?" I asked.

Most nights, after everyone had gone to bed, I crept down the front stairs and dipped deeply into an ice cream carton. I stuffed spoonfuls into my mouth and then smoothed over the icy remains so that no one would notice. Afterward, I tossed in bed and vowed to stop gorging. But the next day I repeated my transgression. I had become a copycat of my father. Each of us was an agent of self-destruction, he for the sake of politics and I in the name of despair.

Perhaps that was the catalyst which prompted me late one night to tiptoe down our front stairs, crawl into the cigar-shaped Hudson my sisters and I called the "Green Hornet," back down our driveway without headlights, and direct the car toward the Kansas Turnpike. It was a deed I executed without any advance preparation other than gathering coins needed for highway tolls. All that I carried was toothpaste, with a brush, and the telephone number of my best friend in Mac, Becky Carson.

Some foggy part of my thinking suggested that the solution to a deep ache, which never seemed to abate, existed out there in the comforting center of Kansas. My heart fantasized that the political and personal winds that had buffeted our family, with my father at the vortex, would stop blowing once I was in the only place completely familiar to me.

After my coins had dropped into the toll basket at the first turnpike booth, the abrupt commitment to living away from my parents and sisters began to gel. Their images flitted by me in the inky interior of the Hudson to taunt my decision. Margo sat with Spot at her feet and stared at me with those transparent blue eyes. Andrea glanced quickly at me, and then away. Mom appeared with her "That's enough" expression. Her eyes ordered me to turn the Hornet around and abandon my ridiculous getaway. I missed them already. I imagined them crying when they discovered my empty bed and speculated about whether an intruder could have spirited me away.

Then an image of my father stepped into the Green Hornet to replace their familiar facades. He was talking. His eyes penetrated mine with the expression that was so difficult to ignore. He had not arrived to reprimand me as my mother would have. He only said, "I love you, Mrs. Tusswagon. Do you love me, too?" He continued looking at me, evidently willing to do so until I answered.

I drove on through darkness as his political declarations rang through the car and bounced off the dashboard. "MYYY FELLL-OH REEE-PUB-LICK-UNS!" His voice trembled. "I INNN-TEND TUH BE GUVVV-UH-NUH." He blew a smoke ring.

Once upon a time, not so long before, my heart had swelled at his political coups. I had believed as surely as he that the governor's chair would have his name inscribed as its occupant. Yet his sweet promises and staunch declarations had begun to waver slowly like candles about to extinguish themselves. No single event had transformed me into a disbeliever. Not the visit to Josie, whose name could be mentioned and still make my heart palpitate and splinter. Not all the moving from place to place either. Nor was it any one of all his excesses, which he swore never to repeat. He and I had never crashed and burned together over a single event or even acknowledged the widening chasm. He even possessed enough of that old charm to weasel his way into a tiny corner of my heart. But most of it had closed off access to him as if blocked by the debris of a multitude of landslides.

* * * * *

As I entered Mac near dawn, fatigue dulled the significance of my flight. I steered the Green Hornet to the Walnut Street curb of Becky's house. It was several doors away from the one with sweeping porches

155

and a stained glass window. Her silhouette loomed large and luminous in the aura of a rising sun. I concentrated on not looking in her direction.

Even so, the days of our old neighborhood gang paraded through my head. I could see us racing up and down on bikes playing cops-and-robbers or building mock forts in the alley. I could smell the rain that made us retreat to someone's porch and pretend we were on a ship at sea. I could even envision the stars under which we had chased and begged our parents for just five minutes more of playtime. Those by-gone days remained as vivid in my mind as if I had reverted to child-hood. All of those magic moments, which had accumulated into tender memories, were central to my core.

At the Carsons' front door, my hand froze on its knocker. How was I going to explain being there, a girl once familiar who had appeared mysteriously on their front steps at daybreak? As I rapped, the sound of metal banging against wood echoed in the stillness.

Eventually, I heard footsteps. "Why Cynthia, what on earth ... ?" Mrs. Carson said as she opened the door.

"Can I stay with you awhile?"

She offered a stricken look before stammering, "Of course, dear." Certainly, I could stay, she repeated. But she needed to advise my parents where I was.

She presented cocoa before going into the next room and shutting the door. Minutes ticked by at a turtle's pace before she appeared to say that my father wanted to talk to me on the phone.

"Hi, Mrs. Tusswagon," he said as calmly as if phoning from next door. He planned to board the first Mac-bound train leaving Kansas City Union Station, he said. "I'm coming to get you and bring you home. We have been so worried about you. I love you. Do you love me, too?"

I heard my mother crying in the background. But she did not ask to speak to me. I wondered whether she was furious, or if some of her tears possibly represented a longing for Mac that she shared with me.

Perry met my father at the train when it arrived at his Mac depot and directed the Packard to the Carsons' curb.

"Mrs. Tusswagon!" He rushed through the front door. Becky and her parents stared, making me feel a stab of embarrassment. He began chattering about trains and Kansas City as casually as if we had all encountered each other on the street and decided to step inside for social chitchat.

* * * * *

Later, across town in Hattie's kitchen, we might have regressed back to the one-time Sunday play performances. Perry sat in his corner next to the rubber bands and pipe cleaners. I was stationed in my mother's former seat, next to a warm cherry pie awaiting my father's consumption. Hattie perched on her stool and gazed at my father with rapt attention. He was pacing and smoking and talking, clearly preoccupied with topics far more monumental than pie.

"There is BIIIIG news," he finally blurted.

"You're moving back to Mac!" Hattie appeared ready to swoon off her stool at the thought.

"No, Mama." Her face fell, like bread dough that had decided to reverse its rise.

"But nearby, Mama."

As I half listened, the image of a moving van pulled up in front of my eyes. In the dining room, Mom stood beside her walnut table as if to protect it from the burly men who would cart it away. My father moved through the background and babbled at them about relocating for political reasons, as if they would care enough to even cast a vote. My mind watched the van leave Mac, stop in Indy, unload, arrive again soon to reload, unload in K-Ceee, arrive once more to ferry our belongings to unidentified destinations. An American flag flapped in the breeze above rotating wheels of the van.

"Lawrence," I heard my father say. That caused me to look up. Why, his home during law school days was located a mere hour away from Topeka and the Capitol, he said. He had longed to return there ever since. He failed to add that I was scheduled to begin attending college there in less than a year. Instead, he advised us that Duuuh Docking was about to announce a run for another two years as governor. So the Republicans were in dire need of a worthy opponent. He waited.

I thought of it but rejected the idea of saying, "Maybe you, Dad?"

There was a title company for sale in Lawrence, he went on while directing his gaze toward Hattie. It was a gold mine of an investment but would require a small loan to swing the deal. He simply could not wait to get back to Kansas, away from Mizzou and Democrats who reminded him of Give-Em-Hell-Harry. Bunch of know-it-all types in that title company he worked for, too. He paused.

Hattie stood up and fingered the ring of keys at her waist. "I'll be right back," she said before turning toward the back hall stairs.

Perry waited until she was out of sight to spew words of advice that, apparently, had been accumulating in his corner. He trotted out his timeworn theory about getting a good job and hanging onto it. The one with The Senator, which had produced that exciting Brown case, was a perfect example, he said. He reiterated his mantra about being thrifty instead of lavishing money on expensive cars and out-of-town apartments. He revisited the importance of stability, a concept that was no longer familiar to me.

"Why would anyone in their right mind want to live anywhere but Mac?" he concluded. His eyes bored into the side of my father's temple.

"Dad, I .... " His voice was defensive.

"Perry, leave the child be." Suddenly, Hattie was in the room.

Act Three of the Sabbath play was well underway. Only the wad of cash was much thicker this time. And it was not Sunday.

* * * * *

158

My father sat behind the wheel of the Green Hornet and conducted his monologue as if we were making a Saturday motor trip through Mac instead of navigating the turnpike back to Kansas City. He interspersed nuggets of supposed wisdom with political commentary between interminable stops at trucker stations for coffee choked with sugar and desserts piled high with ice cream.

Midway through the journey, whose refreshment stops were turning a four-hour trip into six, he justified all of the caffeine and sweets. He announced his new vow of abstinence, which required quantities of sugar to stave off the alcohol cravings.

"I've had a lil' talk with myself, Mrs. Tusswagon," he said. "Time has come to lay off the sauce." He reached out to tweak my cheek. Though my heart had leapt more than once at his allusions to undertaking such an effort, something in the pulsating quality of his voice carried more resolve this time. Newly sober and about to wing back to Kansas, maybe he could prove to be that cat with nine lives once described to me by phone from the Mac hospital. His political dream, which had receded through Indy and K-Ceee like a bright moon blotted out by clouds, might be resurrected after all.

The closer we got to Kansas City, the more Mac intruded in my memory. Josie sprang into consciousness as my father's relentless political discourse proceeded in the background. Politics, her apartment, his deceptions, and her beauty congealed one more time into a lump somewhere inside me. I was conscious of riding beside that deceitful man, and the other fatherly one who had come to rescue me. He was repaying the favor I had enacted for him so often.

I considered whether my newly sober father could still become governor. It was a goal that had forever defined his identity. So I supposed it was possible that he could mobilize once again to try and achieve it.

Whether he did or did not, I felt myself facing a chilling reality. In so many ways, I no longer had any idea who my father was. More than that, it no longer mattered to me whether his dream came true.

* * * * *

As my father grappled with his demons, Annas Brown was reviving hers in Hutch. She had fulfilled her parole obligation to live away from Kansas for two years. The abortionist had moved back to the Sunflower State just as our family was about to do.

This murderess of babies who once asked, "Do I look like the kind of woman who gets excited?" had apparently managed to forget the penalties of such crimes during her absence. Once back home in Hutch, she had begun to abort fetuses with the "treatment" again in her East Fourth Street basement.

Her nasty deeds were destined to bring Annas Brown to the attention of law enforcement authorities some time later. In 1967, she would nearly kill another woman while in the process of destroying one more fetus. Hutchinson authorities would charge her with committing illegal abortion. This time, the patient receiving the "treatment" would be named Mrs. Fern Ward. Her husband would be the one to report to police that Annas Brown had nearly killed his 25-year-old wife.

The incorrigible abortionist would be jailed for her deeds. But she would not have to return to the Industrial Farm for Women.

Before this, though, the murderess was slated to meet up with the Mac attorney who had managed to get her released from that prison. Neither she nor he could seem to jump off their hurtling legal train, which was headed for a horrific crash.

CHAPTER NINE

THE MISTRESS AND THE IRS
1959-1962

"Why, if it isn't Mrs. Tusswagon!" The words rushed at me from a bar stool, through the smoke-clogged din of the Stables. A raucous band competed with collegiate voices swelled by Friday TGIF beers. I could hardly see his face. But the voice was unmistakable.

"Go on and get a seat," I said to a couple of friends. "I'll be right there."

"What are you doing here?" My heart quickened at the sight of a coffee cup on the bar before my father. So far, he had adhered to his vow to abstain from the "sauce."

"Just like my ole college days. Joints like this were popular even when I was in law school." His eyes danced with energy and lingered on the shining ponytails of flirting coeds. "Spent a bit of Hattie's Wheat Money here and there." He reached out to touch my cheek, making me jerk away. "How's school going, Mrs. Tusswagon?"

"Fine." The follow-up rose from my throat unbidden. Its theme was etched on my tongue from years of trying to please him. "What's new on the political front?"

I already knew the answer. My mother had told me that he was spending nearly all of his time in Topeka. She had offered the news in that let's-change-the-subject tone she employed so effectively. He had become a lobbyist at the state Capitol, she said, leaving the details dangling in space as a possibly dangerous disclosure to pursue.

Though his clothes hung in my parents' closet, it did not seem that much else of my father resided in the new house on Wellington Road in Lawrence. I looked for clues of him during frequent visits home from the nearby University of Kansas campus. But these forays were designed more to do laundry or snitch kitchen staples than to learn of his latest pastimes.

His I'm-going-to-buy-a-Lawrence-title-company plan, presented months before in Hattie's kitchen, had not succeeded. He had offered no definitive explanation at its demise except for an airy hand wave that banished the idea off to his stockpile of failed ventures.

I was envisioning him racing about Capitol halls as a frenzied lobbyist when his voice brought me back to the Stables. "Ye Gods, it's a good thing I'm back on the political front in Topeka." He launched into a spirited analysis of the deterioration that had occurred in Kansas politics since his departure as GOP chairman. Why, the Grand Old Party desperately needed a sturdy, unbeatable, knowledgeable, reliable, seasoned, progressive candidate for the next gubernatorial election, he said.

He glanced expectantly at me, as if we were back on Walnut Street and I should say, "Maybe you, Dad?"

"I have to go now. Sorry, Dad. My friends are waiting."

He looked crestfallen, like a child whose mother had said he was about to be spanked.

"One last thing, Mrs. Tusswagon."

My legs dangled off the bar stool, preparing to depart.

"Did your mother mention that I've been thinkin' about buying my favorite Topeka bar? Pickles. Remember the one I always talked about?" He hurried to add that it would just be something to occupy his spare time and bring in cash while he geared up for a political run.

Something crystallized in my memory bank as I sat there among the shrill voices and clank of ice against glasses. It swept me back to the American Legion in Mac where, then as now, my legs had hung in midair and I had longed to escape. I could hear his voice making political pronouncements to his patriotic pals and assuring them that their faith in him would always be justified. The Legion bar metamorphosed in my mind into a series of other darkened liquid caves. All of them meshed into one murky, loud cocoon like the Stables. For as long as I could remember, places like these bars had served as my father's playground and performance stage. Now he wanted to own one of them.

He was still rambling on as I tried to refocus. Politics would be his main undertaking from now on, he said. But he would need to live weekdays in Topeka, rather than Lawrence, to avoid the lengthy commute.

"I am going to get another Topeka apartment," he said as blithely as if announcing a trip to the grocery store.

"An apartment? Dad, I really do have to go now."

"I love you. Do you love me, too?" He leaned toward my face as I turned away.

* * * * *

My thoughts were scrambling like eggs being whisked in a bowl as I fretted in my dormitory bed later that night. I did not want to think about my father or lie awake engaging in the worry, anger and disillusionment that inevitably stalked me after an encounter with him. There was no need anymore to assume my rigid child's pose and wait for the sounds of his Cadillac in our garage or his unsteady feet mounting front hall stairs. I did not have to play the role of his Night Watchman or daytime consort. I reminded myself that he could no longer sway me like a windsock aloft in gentle breezes, or crush me as he had in a pink apartment. Still, I could not erase the sight of him perched on the Stables bar stool. I heard him talking and spinning the same dreams that had drifted throughout my childhood. Then he said, I love you. Do you love me, too?

Ever since I had been old enough to hold scissors and snip paper dolls from glossy sheets or movie star photos from <u>Modern</u> <u>Screen</u> magazine, some part of me had craved the life of an actress. Maybe it was just that I wanted to be someone else in order to step out of the shy veneer that repressed my wild streak. Or perhaps I longed to act because my father started imprinting me as a child to emulate his own youthful ambition, which had been buoyed by his starring roles in school stage productions.

Recently, I had been selected to appear in a university theater production. So my acting dream, unlike his, was alive and luminous. He had chosen to abandon his own aspirations for stage stardom to chase the singular goal of being governor. It made me wonder how he must feel now, having reached the threshold of his political dream only to see it fade like a watercolor painting diluted by excess water. Glimmering somewhere in those liquid remains was the face of Freddie, whose own defeat and turncoat tactics had aborted the goal my father substituted for becoming an actor.

* * * * *

So it was that our family resumed the political rhythms to which we had reverberated during all the years of the GOP chairmanship, the Hall campaign, and a Topeka apartment. My father disappeared for five days of the week, five and one-half really since he departed after Sunday lunch. My mother spent these empty marital stretches by overseeing all family life as if she were widowed or divorced. It was a lifestyle that had long caused me to remark to curious friends, "My father is a politician, you know. My parents have lived this way for years."

Mom may have been used to this arrangement and even welcomed it. But she did not seem to be acclimating well to life in another strange town. At first, she had occupied herself by producing yet another home interior piece de resistance. An ordinary split-level house had quickly acquired her snazzy signature flair. She had installed white carpeting that mandated shoe removal, and a black-and-white tile entry that needed constant polishing. Part of her house, like the all-white living room, looked too impeccable for real people to live there.

Yet her facade resembled a walking, talking version of a nicked rubber band that had been snapped once too often. She delivered monotone sentences and deflected important questions. Perhaps she had become incapable of processing uproarious information anymore. I longed to ask her why my father was operating the Pickles bar if he intended to stay away from alcohol and get back into politics. But I looked at the black of her eyes reflecting onto dark shadows that etched her face and could not ask.

* * * * *

"Guess who I saw in Topeka at the Capitol?" Margo said to my mother and me. She was just in the door from her high school field trip. It was Friday and I had dropped by to wash clothes.

We paid attention when my sister spoke, mainly because of her keen observational skills. I envied that she could remember dates, conversations, names, and other details that slipped past me as if on a greased track headed out of memory. It disgusted me that she could visit someone's home a single time and later describe all of its furniture arrangements, wallpaper colors, drapery styles and sofa slipcovers. My recollections would be a blur. She enthralled my mother with such vivid descriptions. It made me wish I could be the one who was listened to with such absorption.

"Who did you see?" Mom asked, absently.

"Josie. Remember her? Dad's old secretary."

I jerked as if hearing the name of a murdered relative. One more time, I searched my mother's face to mine it for clues about how much she knew.

"JOSIE?" She stopped fussing with food to listen. "What did she say?" She knew that Margo would not mistakenly identify a person even if observed some years before.

My sister proceeded to explain in her do-not-neglect-a-detail fashion. My father had failed to show up, as promised, to chaperone her class around the Capitol. They had waited and waited. Finally, her teacher had let Margo go to a nearby information station to have him paged. En route, she had encountered Josie.

"In the CAP-I-tulll?" My mother made no pretense of composure.

Margo reported that she had asked Josie if she knew where her father might be. "Yes," she had answered before volunteering to go get him.

"AND?"

Soon he came rushing down the hall with some excuse about his lobbying work, Margo said.

Icy silence entered the kitchen to freeze out further conversation. My mother began busying herself with some mindless task. My sister looked stricken, unaware that she had just precipitated Armageddon.

It occurred to me once again that my mother, based on her reaction, might know more about Josie than I had suspected. All of my efforts to avoid the topic of my father and his secretary, and my excruciating guilt about being deceptive, may not have been necessary. Perhaps she had known from the very start about his violation of their elopement vows and decided to endure it.

Maybe her retaliatory thoughts had begun festering that night my father's secretary floated onto our porch in Mac. Or possibly they had started simmering when he had insisted on slaving away, supposedly, at his law office on Saturdays with Josie. If Mom had known about it way back then, she must have felt like he was pouring arsenic into her aged wounds now. Yet how could she have survived this so long if she had been privy to the indignities dumped on her by my father and his pink paramour?

But, of course, she was not about to divulge answers.

I considered the possibilities: Had Josie followed us from Mac to Independence, then Kansas City, and finally Lawrence via Topeka? Had she been playing the role of a silent ghost who haunted our family like Hattie did? Was it possible that my father had been keeping her holed up in pink apartments outside all of our towns, making her wait for his visits so they could drink vodka and do mischief?

My mother chose a frontal attack against her competitor. Margo reported that she launched it during a weekend conversation with our father.

"I understand Josie is living in Topeka," she said with studied casualness.

"Uh … now … " Pushed into a corner from which there was no escape, even his repertoire of creative excuses failed him on this one. A weak "Yes" was all that he could muster.

"Let's invite her for a back yard barbecue," she proposed, miraculously nonchalant.

"Fine. Sure. Okay." He muttered something like that, desperate to change the subject.

* * * * *

I made plans to drop by and observe the face-off after Margo advised me of the date and hour. She confided that Mom had been in a dither as to what patio supper outfit might flatter her most. She had laid skirts and blouses and dresses across her bed and paired them with jewelry and shoes. But she had not fussed with the barbecue menu, as usual, said my sister. Only the clothes seemed to matter.

The prospect of encountering Josie again conjured images of her diaphanous frame with its fluff of cotton-candy hair. I could see her move like a panther as she prowled toward a pink couch. She wore her favorite hue neck to ankle.

She walked up our front steps promptly at 6:30. Josie was still exquisite though a bit plumper. Blonde hair, shorter now, frothed about that milky complexion and across her forehead in soft bangs. Pink had apparently remained her favorite color. She wore it in a cotton dress with a scoop neck and full skirt. Her open-toe high heels matched.

167

"Virginia, you look lovely. And how nice to see you girls again," she said. "Cynthia, why look at you! I haven't seen you since ... " She stopped.

"Hel-OOOh." She addressed my father as if they had not encountered each other for years.

He jingled coins in his pocket and smoothed his balding scalp.

"Let's go out back to the patio," my mother said before twirling around. All of us followed her like a phalanx of newborn ducklings trailing their mama.

"Drink orders?" she asked before we had time to sit down.

"I'll have my usual ... uh ... " Josie looked at my father before he rushed off.

Mom marched immediately into a tide of questions. She sought specifics concerning Josie's whereabouts since we had left Mac and facts about her job history. She even tried to pick for details of her love life. My mother appeared to have metamorphosed from an etiquette-proper hostess to a ruthless detective.

Listening, I glanced back and forth between her and Josie. Each still exuded beauty, though it was slightly eroded by the ravages of time. Josie had been gifted at birth with the type of extraordinary looks that required no enhancement. My mother had not been so fortunate. But over time, she had learned how to package the attributes she did possess into a stylish result.

As I watched Josie reposition her tanned legs and my mother frown at her, thoughts turned to my father and his unquenchable thirst for adoration. Considering that, Josie would seem to have emerged as the winner of these disparate rivals for his affection.

"It's my Tall Paul, the future governor of Kansas," I could hear her sing to him from an apartment balcony. "Politicians are a bunch of phonies," I could recall my mother repeating <u>ad nauseam</u>.

One of them had been wise enough to offer the incessant praise he needed to function. The other had nipped at his deficiencies in hope of transforming him to someone he was incapable of becoming.

I looked once more at my mother, then at Josie. Much as I despised the outcome, I comprehended why his secretary had won. She had recognized that my father was no different from a kitten drawn automatically to rays of comforting sunshine. As long as she was able to fill those rays with unquestioning adulation, he would never stop seeking them.

Suddenly, he came racing back with glasses teetering on a tray as Josie continued trying to field the personal inquisition.

"Virginia, she probably doesn't want to give a blow-by-blow account of her life," he said. He distributed drinks and sat down. His right leg began to jiggle violently as if to detach itself. His eyes darted like spinning yo-yos between his wife and former secretary.

"What did you say you are doing in Topeka?" My mother fixed her best piercing gaze on Josie.

"Now Virginia ..."

"I smell something burning," Mom said, directing daggers at him.

He jumped up and headed toward the grill. Shortly, he returned with a plate of sooty breasts and thighs.

"Oh dear, Tall Paul ... "

"Get the hell out of here, Josie!" Suddenly my mother was on her feet, quivering with rage and advertising a face as black as the chicken soot. "GO! NOW! And never come near us again." Her voice trembled as the fullness of her venom began to spill.

"And you stay right there." She whipped around and leveled a blazing look at my father.

Josie got up, teetering on high heels. She looked uncertain, as if this could all be imaginary.

"You heard me. GO!"

* * * * *

As domestic combat broke out in a back yard of Lawrence, battle of a different sort was soon to be ignited across the state in a Wichita

169

courtroom. Like the marital conflict, this one had been simmering for some time in a stew pot of suspicions and accusations. In each case, the double-crossed party had decided to confront the perpetrator in public.

Just as my mother had declared war on Josie, the Internal Revenue Service was preparing to crack open the Annas Brown parole-for-money political scandal. Like Mom, they were out of patience. The IRS was tired of asking different versions of their question: Who had received the $10,000 parole bribe and failed to pay taxes on it?

Like detectives stalking an elusive murderer, the IRS had been collecting evidence. In late 1958 and early 1959, they had interviewed Mack Nations, Clair Hyter, and Paul Lackie.

They had heard the advice Governor Hall's executive secretary gave to Clair Hyter: "I told him if he had given money to Fred Hall that he had better be sure he wasn't left holding the sack because I wasn't going to be left holding the sack on the thing ... that he had better be worrying about himself because Fred Hall wasn't going to worry about anyone but himself."

They had listened to Paul Lackie describe the Town House meeting and finger his former friend, Fred Hall, as arbiter of whether a $10,000 parole amount would be acceptable: "I told them that I did not know if The Little Man (that is what I and Mack Nations called Fred Hall) would settle for that amount."

And they had heard Clair Hyter suggest that Fred Hall might be paranoid: "...when I was in his office discussing a pardon for Annas Brown he seemed as if he did not care to cooperate or to even discuss the subject. Later Mack Nations told me Governor Hall had acted this way because he was afraid a bug was in his office."

Still, the puzzling question of who got the cash was nearly eight years old. By February of 1962, only one month remained to file an indictment. The statute of limitations on prosecuting tax evasion in this case would expire in late March. After that, whoever siphoned off the money, tax-free, could not be prosecuted.

On February 21st, the IRS filed its indictment. "THE UNITED STATES VERSUS STARLING MACK NATIONS" targeted the governor's one-time executive secretary. The IRS premise was that he had roamed about paying off nearly $5,000 in debts with cash just three days after the parole payoff. And he had never paid taxes on it.

The net cast by the IRS case was cleverly designed to snare additional recipients of the payoff if their complicity could be proven. To ensure this possibility, the grab bag cast of characters who had plotted the bribe was being summoned to appear in Wichita U.S. District Court. Some had to be subpoenaed.

This declaration of war surprised the involved principals, who assumed passing time had sealed their deeds away from exposure. They hardly suspected that their dirty little undertaking, hidden away in a stockpile of political secrets, would erupt. They would have been horrified at the prospect of these details being spilled onto newspaper front pages across a state one of them had governed and another hoped to.

Back when the bribery deal had been designed, a governor who described himself as a "do-something" never fathomed that it could emerge one day as political humiliation. An aspiring governor, who had vowed "I...INNN-TEND TUH BE GUVVV-UH-NUH," hardly dreamt that his political actions would be castigated rather than praised in public. His legal co-partner in the parole effort had not anticipated that his professional conduct would be ridiculed in a courtroom. And the governor's executive secretary had hardly suspected that he would be charged with federal tax evasion.

Certainly, none of them had anticipated that they would be forced to convene in a room with that portly abortionist who starred at the root of this political abscess and whose family money had funded the bribe. They might have laughed if someone had suggested that one day they would have to listen to her describe them as fools instead of the other way around.

171

* * * * *

One key figure in this political morass was not taken by surprise when the IRS filed its case against Mack Nations. Annas Brown had known about the intent for some time. In between her basement abortions, she had complied with a request to appear as a federal witness before a grand jury. It had met before the case against former Governor Hall's executive secretary was filed.

The jury's mission had been to compile documentation concerning the parole bribe prior to the indictment. On that topic, she possessed invaluable information.

On August 7th, 1961, it had also heard testimony from Paul Lackie.

CHAPTER TEN

WHO GOT THE PAYOFF?
1963

Even now, my most vivid impressions of the grim days during that particular May concern my mother. And my sisters. Crystallized vignettes of their agonized faces, and memories of their silent crucifixions, remain lodged in my mind like storm clouds fixed in a black sky.

Each day at the sound of a newspaper plopping on concrete, Mom rushed out the front door to snatch the bundle bound with a rubber band. Indoors, she tiptoed to a closet at the back of the house. Her silent mission was to hide newspaper headlines from Margo, Andrea and me. She did not want us to confront the thick blocks of newsprint screaming about political payoffs and crooked attorneys. Had it occurred to her, she might have used a black marker to cross out my father's name, which spread like tainted blood through front-page articles. She could also have destroyed daily captions such as "NATIONS SAYS SOMEONE LIES" or "GIVEN $10,000 FOR A PAROLE." But she would not have been able to erase the etched creases on her face or the deepening crevasses beneath her eyes.

Margo, who had become a fiercely protective agent to shield Mom from our father's misdeeds, did not mention the absence of newspapers. But his misbehavior was pummeling her, too. The shame descending on our family in the name of his political glory could not have occurred at a more inopportune time. Within days, The Student was scheduled to mount stairs to a high school stage and accept a graduation diploma. She should have been able to hold her head high with pride over exemplary grades. She had already selected fried chicken and chocolate cake for the menu at a family celebration to be held in her honor. Grandma Ida was even driving all the way to Lawrence to attend.

My mother might have been stashing away the daily newspapers in late May. But Margo did not need to read them to sense the scalding glances cast her way by classmates. Not until many years afterward would she confess to us that one of her teachers had made nasty remarks concerning the sins of cheating and politicians who are prone to do so. She would report that he had looked directly at her while castigating such liars.

Instead, Margo said very little during those days of hidden newspapers other than to announce her intent to boycott her fancy class party. She did not need to explain why.

Since I was living away from home, I relied on Margo for daily updates. The phone rang incessantly, she said. Knocks sounded at the front door. No one answered either of them. My mother sobbed into her pillow at night. She wore her "That's enough" look all day.

Margo said she and Andrea ventured into public wearing those trademark phony political faces designed to camouflage heartache. These masks, which Mom taught us to don, had always featured slight smiles to indicate basic contentment. They had never been intended to be false fronts behind which to hide shame about our own scandal-ridden politician. My sister told me that she, Andrea and Mom sat at the table each night like live mannequins moving food about their plates while never mentioning my father's name.

* * * * *

This nightmare had begun as just another political nuisance. My father announced that he was scheduled to travel to Wichita and its courthouse. He claimed to have been summoned for some ridiculous hearing involving his old pal Freddie, and his one-time executive secretary Mack Nations. He treated it with his usual smoke screen technique while muttering about that damnable Brown case, and complaining about turning over Pickles for someone else to operate.

174

He mentioned the IRS but glossed over the part about its filing suit against Mack, as everyone called him. He skipped the aspect of Freddie being subpoenaed from California to appear. And he deleted the tidbit that Annas Brown was scheduled to testify. He also failed to divulge that he had been subpoenaed, too, nearly four months before in late January. And he certainly did not let on that Mack Nations had been arrested in February and released on a $1,000 bond after entering a "not guilty" plea.

Detecting nonchalance on his part, none of us considered his May 20th departure for Wichita as anything more than another obligation to perform our traditional farewell ritual. That he wore a rather haggard expression was not alarming. It matched the countenance my mother had been offering for months.

I happened to be at home during his weekend departure. So I joined the standard leave-taking in the kitchen. My sisters and I milled about. We were eager to be finished with it. I was looking out the window over the sink when he blurted, "I did nothing wrong. I swear to you." I twirled around to see him glancing from one of us to the other. It occurred to me that I might have been daydreaming and missed his reference to exactly what he was accused of doing. Looking at him, I failed to detect guilt on his face or in his eyes. I only saw my perpetual image of the tall and distinguished politician who stood holding a hang-up bag, poised to depart.

"Bye, Dad," someone said.

"Have fun, Dad."

"Bye, Mrs. Tusswagon, Snussy Puss, Doodlebug." He saved my mother for last. "Snooky, I'll be back before you know it. In plenty of time for the graduation."

She wore one of Grandma Ida's flowered aprons and leaned her reed-thin body against the counter. She held a cigarette in one hand and a cup of coffee in the other. Her black eyes were flat like frozen pools into which it would be dangerous to dive. She did not seem to see him or us.

"I love you, Snooky." His eyes beseeched her. "Do you love me, too?"

Watching them, it crossed my mind that she and he probably knew far more than they would divulge to us. My mother was as inscrutable as ever. His "I did nothing wrong" lingered in the air like dank fumes after a chemical spill. Since he had never defined wrongdoing or honesty in the traditional way, the seriousness of whatever was about to happen could be more significant than was being portrayed. He had never viewed lying to Mom, his parents, or us as wrong. Or asking me to do the same. These altered versions of events had always been categorized as fibs rather than lies. He considered them harmless and well-intentioned. So the implications of this Wichita appearance, and my parents' purposeful silence about it, raised one more red flag in a lifetime of them.

* * * * *

The following day, as the IRS court case began Monday morning, important events were unfolding in unrelated settings far away from Wichita.

Down South in Birmingham, Alabama, more than 1,000 students were expelled or suspended from school for their roles in anti-segregation demonstrations. In the East, President John F. Kennedy was scheduled to present astronaut Gordon Cooper with the NASA Distinguished Service medal.

In Wichita, the daily docket at the stately courthouse listed "THE UNITED STATES VERSUS MACK NATIONS" for May 21st. The IRS was accusing the governor's one-time executive secretary of "willfully and knowingly" filing a fraudulent 1956 income tax return.

The selected jurors were seven men and five women. They had called their daily lives to a halt to sit in the handsome jury box and evaluate political misconduct. There were two housewives, a trio of secretaries, a purchasing agent, a cook, a railroad clerk, a seedsman, a utility serviceman, an analyst for an aircraft company, and a tank man for a packing company.

The plaintiff had summoned a stellar cast of political luminaries to appear in the second-floor courtroom, which was resplendent in mahogany and gilt. The intent was to prove that the defendant, who was still boyish-faced at 44, had received nearly half of the $10,000 payoff to parole Annas Brown. Then he had evaded a $1,200 tax payment.

To back up its claim, the IRS had assembled a former governor, a would-be governor and attorney, a murderess, a second attorney, a former state senator, a district judge, a Kansas Bureau of Investigation special agent, and assorted satellite acquaintances of this ensemble.

The prospect of their juicy tales and testimony had attracted a crowd of spectators to hear the details. They wanted to glimpse the live versions of Kansas political celebrities whose photos had appeared in their newspapers. The lurid trial had caused them to cast aside chores of a typical Monday in favor of staring at The Little Man governor, the Peck's Bad Boy bribe plotter, pudgy Mrs. Brown, and the defendant of an impoverished background.

Even the defense attorneys were political notables. Cliff W. Ratner was the son of former Kansas governor Payne Ratner. William Mitchell was a former speaker of the Kansas House of Representatives. The prosecution team had recruited some heavyweights as well. Assistant U.S. Attorneys Thomas Joyce from Kansas City and Robert Green of Wichita were representing the IRS.

Judge J. Arthur Stanley Jr. had traveled from Kansas City, Kansas, to preside over the case. He advised the jurors that he wanted a speedy trial. He needed to travel to the East Coast toward week's end. Apparently, he did not anticipate how confounding the testimony that loomed would be. It was going to take some time to sort out a surreptitious deed involving abortions, dirty money, lies, and political favors for which no participant was about to take the rap.

* * * * *

There was a crisis at the outset. Annas Brown, who had been subpoenaed by federal agents, failed to appear on the morning of the trial's Day One. Attorney Joyce told Judge Stanley: "Well, the government doesn't know where she is and she was supposed to report."

"If you need any assistance in obtaining her appearance, you let me know," the judge said. "This court has full power to enforce the subpoena if any further action is required."

So the proceedings began without her. Later in the day, she finally showed up. The abortionist was apparently as unexcited about this trial as she had been her own.

Mack Nations was profiled by his attorneys first. They chronicled his rise out of poverty in Greensburg, Kansas, after his father had died when he was 11. Attorney Ratner described how his client and widowed mother had struggled to make ends meet by operating the family's weekly newspaper. Finances were so tight that he even had to quit high school for a year to support his mother and two sisters.

During those times of scarce money, he had developed a strong preference for cash transactions. His inclination had intensified following his family's financial losses in a bank failure. It had caused him to keep cash in safe deposit boxes. He had about $4,000 stored in such a box at the time he paid off the debts being questioned by the IRS, his attorney said.

During World War II while in the Navy, he had managed to save $750 and bought a weekly newspaper in Chase, Kansas. Later, he had sold it at a profit and acquired several other papers before going to work for the governor. Now he was a journalist and employed as oil editor of the Wichita Eagle newspaper.

"Mr. Nations is no lawyer," Attorney Ratner told the jury. "He is a man who started from nothing and built himself up to be one of the leading newspaper publishers in Kansas. A man who is a criminal is not going to do that." Besides, only a governor and the Kansas Parole Board possessed the power to grant pardons or paroles, he pointed out.

Mr. Nations, as a mere executive secretary, had no clout to influence a prison release, he said.

Next came a parade of character witnesses to laud Mack Nations. They depicted the defendant as an industrious, honest, ethical, church-going, devoted-to-his-mother man. They could not seem to halt the superlatives that spilled from their tongues.

Yet the central problem remained: If the accused had not received $4,900 of the $10,000 bribe, why did he rush off three days after accepting the envelope of money to satisfy nearly that amount of debt in cash? He had applied his money to several outstanding financial obligations. About $3,700 of it had helped satisfy a bank debt. Over $500 had been designated for a sum owed the Sunflower Publishers Company, where he was a stockholder. The remaining $600 had been split evenly between a real estate loan debt and his Congregational Christian Church.

In order to position their client as innocent, the Nations legal team zeroed in on former Governor Fred Hall. He was the person the IRS was actually out to get instead of his client, Attorney Ratner told the jury. "They tried to get Hall, but they failed, and so they got Mack Nations," he said. "The Treasury Department has been after Hall since 1955 or 1956." He referred to the ongoing investigation of the former governor's tax returns for those years. He also noted that it was Fred Hall who had authorized his executive secretary to attend the April first parole powwow at Attorney Lackie's apartment.

"Was it your custom to enter into meetings as to the parole of prisoners?" Attorney Green asked Mack Nations.

"If I had known those people were to be there, I assure you I would not have gone," he answered. He had not even known the purpose of this meeting, he said.

Mack Nations, who had been just 36 years old when chosen as executive secretary, said he told his boss after the meeting that it would be "bad politics" to parole Annas Brown. "It seemed to me a political error to parole her, and I so stated." He also testified that he had made

179

similar comments at the Town House apartment gathering to plan the parole. "I said that a great deal of political hay would be made if she asked for a parole and didn't get it."

He did admit talking with the governor about the Town House get-together. Attorney Lackie had asked him to do so, he said. "As far as I remember, I started to tell him (the governor) about meeting with Lackie, and he interrupted me before I finished. And he said something like 'Tell him we'll take care of the matter,' or 'It will be taken care of.'"

"Whatever he said, I called Paul Lackie and told him."

Not long after that, he had carried out the governor's orders to fire Attorney Lackie as legal counsel of the Kansas Corporation Commission, he said. The dismissal was because of the nature of the April Fools' Day meeting.

Upon learning that Annas Brown was going to be released from prison, he had warned his boss a second time about the bad politics and possible consequences of it, Mack Nations said. "The governor told me, 'You're wrong' and handed me a typewritten note from Jack Harris, publisher of the Hutchinson News." The governor had asked the publisher to check around Hutch to see if there would be negative reaction to a Brown parole. The governor claimed that his research had concluded there would be no backlash related to her release.

As all of this had been occurring between the governor and his executive secretary, their professional relationship was deteriorating. "A falling out," Mack Nations said in describing it. "He did something then that as far as I know never had been done by a governor before. He closed the door between his office and mine, and that also included the office of his private secretary, Barbara Harwi." That move prevented the direct access to the governor's office he had previously enjoyed, he said. "From then on, I had to call the secretary or the governor and ask if I could come in. We lost complete communication almost immediately." It had also caused a "very unfriendly" feeling between him and Barbara Harwi.

He had been just a few months into his job when the governor fired him, Mack Nations recalled. He was told that he could stay on the job until June. But his boss had failed to explain why he was being let go.

In prior testimony to federal agents, Mack Nations had been unable to recall who asked him to wait for a delivery at the Capitol office that fateful Saturday. "That was some years ago and I don't remember exactly," he had told them. "I think it may have been the governor who told me to stay, or it might have been his private secretary. Clair Hyter told me recently he had called and asked me to wait. I know someone told me to wait there."

He did remember, vividly it seemed, details of that bulging envelope of money. "I didn't open the envelope," he insisted. Whenever such materials arrived during the governor's absence, he had locked them in his desk drawer until they could be delivered, he said. He had done precisely that with this one, too.

"Did Hyter say anything to you when he handed you the envelope?" Attorney Ratner asked.

"It has been awhile, and I don't remember exactly. He could have said something like, 'Here is the envelope for the governor' or 'This is what you have been waiting for.'"

Attorney Joyce belittled Fred Hall by painting an imaginary scenario of the former governor okaying the parole deal. He based his depiction of the dialogue on the fact that Mack Nations had reportedly said as he left the Town House apartment parole meeting that he would return to the Capitol and discuss the payoff with the governor.

He suggested, with thinly veiled sarcasm, that the executive secretary had been instructed to discuss the amount of the payment with "the Little Man which they called Governor Hall, and ostensibly Governor Hall was to get this money at that time . . . Finally, the Little Man said they could go get her (Brown), and they got the money and headed for the penitentiary."

When Mack Nations finally completed his version of events of the parole payoff day, Attorney Hyter mounted the stand to reconstruct his recollections. They would portray an entirely different envelope story.

First, he darted and danced around specifics of that day. He was already aware that Mack Nations had fingered him as a payoff recipient during conversations with federal agents preceding the trial. He knew that Fred Hall had also targeted him as the bribe benefactor.

His re-creation of the payoff delivery events was then presented: "I handed him (Nations) the envelope," he said.

"What did he say?" asked Attorney Joyce.

"Very little."

"What did you say to him?"

"I told him I had some additional expenses because of the delays. I asked him for $200."

"Then what did he do?"

"He opened up the package and gave me $200."

"What did he do with the balance?"

"He put it in the inside drawer of his desk."

Yet in statements given to federal and state agents prior to the trial, he had not referred to the envelope being opened or receiving his requested $200. Pressed now for the truth pertaining to mismatched stories, he said the version involving an opened envelope was the correct one. Some time later, he would admit: "I've made some contradictory statements to revenue agents that Nations opened and did not open an envelope containing the money."

To further confuse the jurors, Attorney Hyter said that Mack Nations had asked him in 1957, and again in 1958, to report the $10,000 on an amended 1956 income tax return so the IRS would drop an investigation into the matter. He had agreed to do so and paid about $3,200 in taxes in 1959. "I stipulated that I did not receive the money," Clair Hyter said. He had considered himself a transmittal agent and filed for a refund, he added.

"Did you ever discuss the matter of reporting the $10,000 with anyone else?" Attorney Joyce asked.

"I think I may have discussed it once with Governor Fred Hall."

Throughout his legal dealings with the Brown family, he had repeatedly advised that their payoff money was intended for Governor Hall, Clair Hyter insisted.

The finger pointing continued as Attorney Ratner read a statement the Hutch attorney had made earlier to Treasury agents regarding a meeting of him and Mack Nations. It had taken place in Newton, Kansas, near Hutch. At the get-together, Clair Hyter had pinpointed Fred Hall as the payoff recipient.

He recalled, "During my conversations with Nations in Newton, he told me Hall said he would never admit he received the $10,000, that he would not have anything like that in his record because he was undergoing a security check in connection with a job in California."

Also on the courtroom agenda was the attorney who had masterminded the parole bribe. Before he strolled across the room, he was no doubt fidgeting with one shaking leg. Yet his nervousness would vanish, and his voice would not tremor once he began addressing the courtroom. His years of confronting political crowds, large and small, ensured that.

Asked his profession, Attorney Lackie described himself to the court as "an attorney then of McPherson, now of Topeka and Lawrence." Then he proceeded to lead jurors, judge, attorneys, and spectators through a maze of recollections. They were so vague and conflicting that a frustrated Attorney Joyce finally pronounced him "a reluctant witness."

As the Topeka Daily Capital noted on its front page the following day:

> "Joyce had some difficulty getting Lackie to fix
> dates and places of some conversations ... "

Attorney Joyce and others in the courtroom were not accustomed to this normal repartee of a man who might suggest on a political podium that two and two added up to five. Or tell his wife that he was flush with money when their bank account was overdrawn. They could not

183

appreciate the fact that his supposed political pal had turned on him. Or that brain cells killed by alcohol were apt to scramble his thoughts concerning past and present.

So they could hardly be blamed for getting lost in his confusing contentions on topics like the Brown parole payoff. Addressing the issue of that dirty money, he said that he had mentioned a legal fee of $1,500 to the family when they hired him to represent the abortionist. He had been practicing law in McPherson at the time.

Before and after the 1954 election, he had talked with Governor Hall about his client and her desire to be paroled, Attorney Lackie said. But then Mack Nations had informed him that any cases he had should be discussed with him, not the governor. Prior to the Town House meeting, he had informed Mack Nations that he was seeking the Brown parole.

"Now, what did Mr. Nations tell you?" asked Attorney Joyce.

"He told me that Annas Brown had considerable funds in reserve."

"Did he tell you where those funds were?"

"Yes, Commerce Trust Company, to the best of my recollection, in Kansas City."

"And what else did he tell you?" continued Attorney Joyce.

"Only that he felt that the fee upon which I had tentatively agreed was not large enough and should be $25,000," said Attorney Lackie.

Yet the governor's executive secretary had left the ultimate monetary decision to him, claimed Attorney Lackie. "Nations in effect said it was my case and he didn't know why I was discussing it with him ... it was up to me to set the fee. He said he would check on the matter to see what could be done." He had left the apartment meeting "presumably to check with that little man, the governor," said Attorney Lackie. Later, he had telephoned to say that the parole proposition was acceptable to Governor Hall.

Conflicting answers to the question of who was to get what part of the bribe surfaced during this testimony. Attorney Lackie first said that the entire amount was to be paid to him, with dispersal not yet determined. Later, he admitted that division of the payoff had been discussed prior to the Town House confab and he expected to collect $5,000. The governor and his executive secretary were to split the rest and net $10,000 each.

Attorney Joyce, who was already losing patience with this witness's testimony, pressed him for specifics of his discussions with Mack Nations. In return, he got another of those zigzag explanations:

"The governor's pardon and parole attorney was to have some registered cattle, to the best of my recollection for a ranch he had, and the governor and Mr. Nations and I were to share in the fee. To the best of my recollection no specified amounts were designated."

Once the former GOP chairman had finally concluded his testimony, Judge Stanley announced that jurors and trial principals would be sequestered that evening until 9:30. He advised them to get a good night's sleep following dismissal because he might continue until 11 the next night. His intent was to wrap up the case by Wednesday.

* * * * *

Day Two of the trial resumed at 9:30 sharp. Barely 12 hours after they had disbanded, weary jurors were back in court to digest more confusing testimony.

Down South in Alabama, Governor George Wallace was defying federal desegregation orders to enroll two black students at the University of Alabama. Overseas, the United States and the West European Common Market were about to reach a compromise after six days' negotiations to trim world trade barriers.

Such global crises were of marginal interest to me at a time when my father's name marched across newspaper front pages with black type replicating that of international reports. Perhaps it was inevitable that after years of my father's passion for newspapers and words, I had gravitated into journalism for a career. Like him, I found it impossible to discard newspapers without reading them front to back. Stacks of unread dailies always lay in a corner of my bedroom awaiting examination.

So it was that as my father fidgeted in a Wichita courtroom on May 22nd, I stood at a campus newsstand eyeing the reading possibilities. Instinct advised me that I should not rush over to glance at banner headlines on Kansas City, Topeka, Wichita and Lawrence papers. I knew that I should avoid the information my mother was hiding in a closet at home.

Yet even from a short distance, I could see "HALL DISCLAIMS PAROLE PAYOFF" parading across a Wichita paper propped up at the counter. I ventured closer, drawn like Cleopatra to the poison of her viper.

"NATIONS LISTS ADVICE TO HALL ABOUT PAROLE" bugled the Lawrence newspaper's headline. Relief that my father's name was not featured in it coursed over me. I handed the salesman a coin, snatched the Lawrence paper, and tried not to run to a corner and start reading.

Instantly, my eyes gravitated to block letters in parentheses below the front page fold. Paragraph six of column two read:

"(EDITOR'S NOTE: Lackie's address is currently listed as 1010 Wellington Rd. in Lawrence)." The paragraph above it quoted Mack Nations: "The governor said something to the effect to tell him (attorney Paul Lackie) we would take care of it, or something like that."

Chunks of despair, like those generated on a pink apartment day, sank to the bottom of my stomach. I read the story over and over. I had to remind myself that this was my father about whom some newspaper reporter was writing. The conniving person being described in newsprint was not someone else's dad who seemed to have discarded the concept of right and wrong. He belonged to me. I stared at his name and our address.

Still, I could not seem to digest the surreal quality of his deed, which had catapulted our family into free fall. I closed my eyes and saw individual vignettes of my sisters and parents at the dinner table. My father sat at one end comparing broccoli to a roadside weed and making us laugh. My mother sat at the other and lectured Margo about fibbing after she had tried to blame someone else for dirt on her yellow shorts. Then Margo asked to be excused so she and Andrea could go play. My youngest sister stood up and waited to escape with her.

I sorted the vignettes like playing cards before trying to assemble them as a total ensemble around the dining room table. But one person always refused to cooperate and complete the picture. Margo glared in my father's direction and left. Andrea exited in her shadow. My mother uttered some expletive against politics and excused herself. I kept calling them to come back in order to patch everyone together. But they did not, and I was the only one left at the table with my jabbering father.

* * * * *

In Wichita, the appearances of a pair of disparate Sunflower State characters as star witnesses were on tap.

The Little Man had returned to Kansas from Long Beach, California, thanks to a subpoena. He had moved west in 1958 after resigning from the Supreme Court to make one final and futile gubernatorial bid in which he was defeated in the primary by Clyde M. Reed. At trial time, he was executive vice-president of the California World's Fair. Prior to that, he had hopscotched jobs. He had been an executive with Aerojet General Corporation, worked at a Los Angeles law firm, and served as president of the California Republican Assembly in 1962.

On the trial's opening day, he had professed innocence before ever appearing on the witness stand by issuing a prepared statement to cement his lack of involvement. It stated: "I am here as a government witness to testify in the trial of Mr. Nations for failure to report income involving an incident while he was serving as one of my executive secretaries ... I am cooperating fully with the government in this case. I am not a defendant in the case, and of course, I did not receive any money in the alleged payoffs."

With that as supportive ammunition, he stepped up to testify. No one mentioned during his introduction that he had been under investigation by the IRS for some time. They suspected him of tax evasion, too.

The one-time governor seemed as feisty as ever. He was also as adamant as in his published statement that he had never received parole money or political contributions from the Brown family.

"Did anyone ever discuss giving you any money for a pardon or parole for Annas Brown?" Attorney Joyce asked.

"No, sir."

The attorney repeated the same question five times, worded in varying ways. Each time, the former governor said, "No, sir."

These curt responses irritated Judge Stanley. He stopped the proceedings to admonish Fred Hall for furnishing less than complete answers.

The former governor said that he had never discussed the parole of Annas Brown with Clair Hyter, though they had met regarding a pardon. His December 1956 meeting with Attorney Hyter had occurred when retired District Court Judge Karl Miller brought the Hutch lawyer to see him. The judge had formerly served as the governor's pardon and parole attorney. Fred Hall said he had advised Clair Hyter that his failure to make proper application for a pardon made talk of one premature.

During one of the governor's two meetings with Attorney Lackie about the Brown parole, a legal fee of $5,000 had been brought up, Fred Hall recalled. "He (Lackie) mentioned he was getting some money, and I assumed he was."

He also seized the opportunity to diminish his one-time friend. "Mr. Lackie had been associated, in reputation and politics, with me, and when I assumed office in January of 1955 he asked for a job and was put on the legal staff of the Corporation Commission ... He came into my office a great number of times ... inquiring as to the possibility of getting a parole for Mrs. Brown. I could only describe Mr. Lackie's presence in the governor's office on several of those occasions as being very difficult to handle."

Despite such conversations, the former governor portrayed his own conduct as impeccable. He had absolutely no advance knowledge of a parole or pardon payoff, the one-time governor said. And he had never received political contributions from Annas Brown.

He volunteered the information that he had decided to dismiss Paul Lackie from his appointment as legal counsel for the Kansas Corporation Commission due to his involvement in the parole matter plus "another incident which occurred in the Corporation Commission."

But he sidestepped the question of why he had fired Mack Nations just a few months into his job. "We reached an understanding for him to leave office in June of 1955." It had nothing to do with any parole payoff, he claimed. That rendition of the firing conflicted with a pretrial statement he had made: "I discharged this man (Nations) over this (failure to report income tax) and other incidents."

Of course, he had not even been in Topeka when the parole money arrived at his office. He had been in Colorado performing gubernatorial duties from August 19th to 23rd, having been asked to speak for a Kansas Day event in Manitou Springs. So how could he possibly have told Mack Nations to wait for Clair Hyter that particular Saturday?

As the former governor concluded his testimony, Attorney Joyce revealed his distrust of the "Little Man." He refused to excuse him as he had prior witnesses. Instead, he requested that Fred Hall remain until the trial had been completed.

Now that testimonials had been made by Annas Brown's two attorneys, a governor she presumed would receive her money, and his executive secretary, the abortionist stepped into the spotlight. Whether she intended to or not, the murderess provided a bit of comic relief.

Evidently, she was no longer grateful that Attorney Lackie had managed to spring her from prison. Shortly after stepping up to the witness stand in a beige suit, she began to belittle him. She started by painting details of his prison visit to her. It had not been a social call. He had traveled to seek her agreement to the bribe sum. The only parole amount he had mentioned was $25,000, Annas Brown said. "I told him he was crazy."

Then she replayed the events of Saturday, August 20th. She might as well have been depicting scenes from a poorly written screenplay. That morning, she had been called to her prison superintendent's office and told she would be released within hours. Before long, Attorney Hyter had shown up and escorted her to freedom.

It was her account of the service station scenario that resembled a scene no competent screen writer would have considered. She described piles of $100 bills being counted by Clair Hyter and stashed in his briefcase, and travelers checks stuffed into his pocket.

Her depiction of an agitated Clair Hyter, pacing a service station restaurant in his business suit, was devastating. "He was so nervous he couldn't sit down and drink a Coke with the rest of us. He kept walking around in the aisles," the portly matron recalled. "He said he had to meet Governor Hall before two p.m."

"And he said he was going to give the money to the governor?" Attorney Joyce asked.

"Yes, sir."

"That was Fred Hall?"

"Yes, sir."

"And you understood all the time that the money you raised was for the governor?"

"Yes, sir."

"Is that the impression you were under?"

"Yes, sir."

Asked whether she had seen an envelope, she said, "No, sir."

190

Annas Brown continued to ridicule Attorney Hyter. She had repeatedly contacted him from her temporary home in Tennessee about whether it would be possible for her to return to Kansas before the two year out-of-state parole stipulation expired, she said. He told her each time that it would be impossible because of too many potential protests.

She also implied that he was a crook. Her family had understood that he could arrange a pardon for her before Governor Hall left office, she said. All they had to do was pay $5,000 following her prison release. She had contacted him frequently from Tennessee about that possibility, too. "I made many calls to Hyter about a pardon," she said. "He said he wasn't sure when he could get it."

During their subsequent conversations, she said her attorney had advised that "he thought he would have a better chance (for a pardon) with Governor Docking."

"Did you ever get it?" Attorney Joyce asked.

"No, sir," she answered in an emphatic voice.

After Annas Brown relinquished her captive audience, Mack Nations returned to the stand. Attorney Green used the opportunity to probe his theory of culpability in the payoff.

"One or the other of you, then, is lying about what you have testified on the stand here?"

"I would say that was the way it is."

"Is it your opinion that Hyter lied from the witness stand?" Attorney Green asked.

"I think he did. There is no question that one of us did."

The attorney also sought information about the Town House apartment rented by Attorney Lackie and the activities conducted there. He suggested that it might have been under "constant control" by Governor Hall or someone in his office as a site used "for the purpose of collecting fees to be used by the governor."

He also zeroed in on the April Fools' meeting and asked whether

Mack Nations had attended it with the intent of discussing formation of a corporation. "Did you, Al Becker, Dave Carson, Paul Lackie and Fred Hall discuss forming a corporation for the purpose of securing fees for subsequent use and in regard to the forming of this corporation, rent rooms to which you went on or about April 1, 1955?"

"The answer is no there, but let me tell you that we did it. But Fred Hall wasn't there. The rest of us talked about forming the corporation. Fred Hall was divorced from his political headquarters. There were contributions coming in regularly, or should have been. We did not want that money going to Governor Hall. He said don't give it to political headquarters. And we discussed the money. It was not Fred Hall. It was Dave Carson, Al Becker, Paul Lackie and myself. The possibility of forming a corporation that would go into that, keeping it away from the governor's office."

"Was the corporation ever formed?" Attorney Green asked.

"If it was, I never knew about it."

"You would have known about it, wouldn't you, as the executive secretary to the governor?"

"Well, I would have if they had told me, but the lawyers were going to take care of it, and that was the last I heard of. I don't think it was."

He added, "During the campaign, Mr. Hall had an apartment there. He held it until well after taking office."

"As executive secretary, I think I would know," he concluded. "But there were lots of things I should have known that I didn't."

Nine defense witnesses made appearances before Day Two of the trial finally concluded after 9:30 that night. Two of them offered parole details. William R. Barker, the Industrial Farm for Women's chief of records, and Annas Brown's daughter Lucille furnished those tidbits.

Six character witnesses followed them in a final attempt to enhance Mack Nations's credibility. One was R. M. Long, retired managing editor of the Wichita Eagle and Beacon newspapers, who praised Nations's "excellent reputation" as an employee.

Wendell F. Cowan, a special agent of the Kansas Bureau of Investigation, also testified regarding his 1956 assignment to look into parole specifics by Governor John Anderson Jr., who was attorney general at the time. The agent said he had interviewed several individuals connected with the parole but had not been directed to take formal statements from them.

One other interesting nugget of information came from IRS agent Marvin C. Jordan. He told of various meetings held with Mack Nations, Clair Hyter, and Fred Hall between 1957 and 1962. He said that he supported the former executive secretary's claims about not opening the payoff envelope and passing it on to Fred Hall. Nations's account of events had remained consistent throughout, he said.

* * * * *

Though Tuesday visits to Wellington Road were rare, I made one late that afternoon. From the exterior, our modest house looked unchanged. Small bushes surrounded the foundation. A large tree bore lush leaves that summer heat would soon come to shrivel.

My key rattled in the front lock of a door that did not creak like the one had in Mac. Standing on the black-and-white hall tile, I thought of that house where the front door had always stood open on a warm afternoon. Spring sounds would tumble through the screen door to mingle with happy ones in the kitchen. The front hall, with its braided rug atop a shiny wood floor, had felt like summer compared to the winter chill of this one.

At first, I assumed no one was home. Then I heard muffled noises traveling down the stairs. I tiptoed closer. Someone was sobbing behind the door of an upstairs bedroom. The sounds sent me back to Walnut Street and school day afternoons when Margo, Andrea and I would troop into a silent house. Our mother had not cried out loud in her darkened bedroom back then. She had just retreated from us into her own private world.

Uncertain what to do, I heard another key in the lock. In came Margo. She wore a frown on a face usually wreathed in a sweet smile.

"It's Mom." I glanced up the stairs. My sister nodded as if nothing was awry. "I don't know what to do," I said.

She put her stack of school books on the bottom stair and headed up.

Watching her retreating back, I considered my family. My father was being castigated in newspapers state-wide. My mother lay weeping bitterly, off in that private sanctuary of hers. Margo was trying to soothe her, as usual. Andrea was away somewhere. And I stood in a cold, dark entryway as if struck dumb and mute.

* * * * *

By Wednesday, May 22nd, the trial was laboring into Day Three. In Birmingham, Alabama, the situation was not a happy one either. Governor Wallace was threatening to bar, personally, any black students who tried to enter the University of Alabama. Meanwhile, President Kennedy was talking of using U.S. troops and marshals to achieve integration.

All over Kansas, newspapers were continuing front-page reports of the parole scandal.

In the Hutch courtroom, the time had come for closing remarks by the lawyers. U.S. Attorney Joyce used the opportunity to toss scathing accusations at Mack Nations and Attorney Hyter: "He (Nations) got a telephone call to come over to the Town House apartments to meet some people. He didn't inquire who they were. He ran right over to the family of an abortionist who wanted to get out of prison. They talked right in his presence about a $25,000 fee to get her out. He didn't say 'that's bribery. My God, I won't have anything to do with it.' When a $10,000 figure was mentioned, he was the messenger boy to carry the offer to the little man, Fred Hall, the governor."

194

Once he had arrived back at the Capitol, the attorney suggested, "He didn't say 'Governor, they are trying to bribe you,' not a word out of his mouth. He calls them back and said the $10,000 would be all right." As for the money delivery: "When he (Nations) was waiting there, he knew there was a $10,000 bribe coming in that office on Saturday afternoon."

An envelope bulging with one-hundred $100 bills "makes a pretty good bundle," Joyce told the jurors. He challenged them as to whether they would be able to handle such an envelope and not suspect that it contained more than a letter or message for the governor.

Attorney Green, a former Kansas state representative, attacked the reputations of both Governor Hall and his executive secretary. The Hall administration had been rotten from the outset, he suggested. "Mack Nations was with that administration from the beginning. A person cannot in three months become that corrupt without going in that corrupt."

Then came the defense team's turn. Attorney Mitchell stepped up to attack Clair Hyter. "Hyter paid the tax that was due on that $10,000 in an amended return. Now Hyter is a lawyer. I just can't imagine a lawyer paying the tax on money for which he says he was only serving as the transmittal agent unless he actually received it."

Mack Nations's behavior during the bribery arrangements was a routine procedure, according to Attorney Mitchell. He said it would not have been at all unusual for his client to attend a conference at the Town House apartments because such meetings were frequently held there or at local hotels. Nor would it have been atypical for him to accept an unidentified envelope for the governor because numerous papers and packages came to him daily for his boss.

Attorney Mitchell suggested that the entire case before the jury was "a political matter." Government attorneys had failed to prove that Mack Nations received any of the $10,000 payoff. He buoyed his contention by recalling the prior court testimony of a trio of Kansas bankers, plus other character witnesses, on Mack Nations's behalf. "His character is so good that they were willing to lend him money on a phone call," he said.

Attorney Ratner pointed out that his client, "who has built himself into one of the leading newspapermen in Kansas," had cooperated fully with the government. The prosecution had based its case on "innuendos and associations without actually furnishing proof of its allegations."

As for his client's former boss, Governor Fred Hall: "Hall was a controversial figure in Kansas politics," Ratner said. "He was hard to get along with."

The defense attorney saved his most ominous remarks for attorneys Lackie and Hyter. Attorney Ratner advised the jury to disregard all testimony by them. He was particularly hard on the Hutch attorney, whom he described as a "lawyer who took money from Annas Brown in the penitentiary and failed to give it back to her." He said, "He's told several conflicting statements."

He attempted to implant his pivotal point by saying, "Only one person in this investigation of Fred Hall has consistently told the same story. That person is the defendant."

Once opposing arguments were completed that afternoon, jurors departed the courtroom at 3:22 to debate the destiny of Mack Nations. Around 5, they were interrupted by Judge Stanley. He needed to advise them of his impending departure for a conference, and that their deliberations should resume at 9:30 the following morning. Judge Wesley E. Brown of the U.S. District Court would replace him and preside over their verdict, said Judge Stanley.

* * * * *

On Thursday morning, May 24th, jurors reassembled at 9:30 to continue, as instructed.

Though Day Four of the scandal continued to merit front-page

196

newspaper coverage, the desegregation standoff in Alabama did, too. President Kennedy and Governor Wallace were still skirmishing over the enrollment of black students. And on the other side of the world, two American mountain climbers had made history. They had accomplished the feat of scaling Mt. Everest and meeting each other at a southern summit.

In the Wichita courthouse, 10 o'clock turned into 10:30. Then 11 chimed somewhere in the building. Finally, at 11:22, jurors filed back into the courtroom. Asked if they had reached a decision, Wichita purchasing agent and jury foreman Clifford Bowman said that they had. The fragile silence of a courtroom, which awaited a crucial decision, prevailed. The foreman passed the verdict to Judge Brown, who asked whether it had been unanimous. The jurors, who had reached their decision on a single ballot, nodded or replied affirmatively.

Starling Mack Nations, they had decided, was not guilty. "There was no question in our minds that something had gone on," foreman Bowman said. "We just didn't think that the government had proved that Mr. Nations got the money."

The verdict prompted the accused to break down and put his head in his hands. He removed his horn rimmed glasses and wiped his eyes with a handkerchief. With shaking hands, he gripped the arms of his chair. After composing himself, he rose and waved aside newspaper reporters to approach the jury box. There he shook hands with each person who had decided his destiny.

An elated Attorney Ratner said, "There was never any doubt in my mind that Mack was innocent. Other witnesses for the government who testified gave contradicting statements. In a not-so-subtle nod to the parade of parole payoff participants who had offered conflicting accounts of what actually happened, Ratner added, "A man that doesn't lie doesn't change his story."

Mack Nations's professional future as a newspaper editor appeared somewhat in doubt as the trial concluded. He said that he had been referred to as "an ex-employee" of the <u>Wichita Eagle</u> in recent accounts of the trial. An innocent verdict had not ended Mack Nations's ordeal with the IRS either.

After the trial's completion, the IRS announced that it intended to conduct further investigation into whether he still owed income tax. The defendant's victory was a sore loss for Attorney Joyce. This was his first defeat after a stunning 36 consecutive convictions.

One might have assumed, based on the trial's outcome, that no one had received the $10,000 payoff. That thick stack of bills, earned by blood extracted by an abortionist, might as well have vanished with nary a trace. All of the cunning and conniving had added up to zero.

* * * * *

As scandals tend to do, this one disappeared from the newspapers but was not forgotten. Subsequent backlash caused by the bribery mess did not bode well for attorneys Hyter and Lackie.

Kansas Attorney General William M. Ferguson had stated during the trial that he was closely watching its developments in case state action might be warranted. Once it had concluded, he requested a trial transcript. He expressed particular interest in statements made by Annas Brown's former attorneys while they were on the witness stand. "There is a possibility of unethical conduct on the part of one or more of the attorneys who testified," he said. He declined naming these individuals when asked to do so.

Yet the media failed to mirror Ferguson's sensitivity: "... he (Ferguson) is interested in statements made by attorneys Clair Hyter, Hutchinson, Kan., and Paul Lackie, Lawrence, Kan., while they were on the witness stand in the federal court trial here" reported the <u>Wichita Eagle</u> on its front page.

U.S. District Attorney Newell George indicated that he also planned to review trial records for possible perjury charges.

The sordid case, which embraced a governor who had once held the state's most prestigious office, an attorney who had been considered his successor, an abortionist who had bought her way out of prison despite butchering a woman and fetus — a case emanating rottenness, greed, and corruption — shook many Kansans' belief in clean government and trustworthy leaders.

One citizen wrote a troubled letter to the <u>Topeka</u> <u>Daily</u> <u>Capital</u>. It featured his comments on the editorial page under a caption: "SOME NAGGING QUESTIONS."

"Why do Kansas citizens have to rely upon federal agencies to uncover such goings-on?" was the first of nine questions.

"Is this an isolated incident?" was another.

The newspaper also ran a devastating Sunday editorial tied to our family's political and personal ordeal. They titled it: "JOLT FOR KANSAS MORALITY."

Among its observations about a trial that they described as "of prime interest to Kansans the past week" were:

> "Mack Nations, one-time executive secretary to former Gov. Fred Hall, has been tried and acquitted of income tax evasion. Understandably he walked happily from the courtroom in Wichita after his acquittal in a trial which was of prime interest to Kansans the past week.
>
> But the trial left more than one question unanswered and left Kansans with the uneasy feeling that some highly questionable practices have been followed in the Statehouse in past years.
>
> The obvious truth is that, after all evidence was submitted in the Nations trial, someone was not telling the truth …
>
> To put it mildly, someone is mistaken. Nations himself testified that he thought the lawyer (Hyter) had lied on the witness stand. 'There is no question that one of us

199

did,' Nations said … Aside from the income tax charges involved in the Nations case, there is the allegation of bribery. It's a distasteful contention to contemplate that money can open the doors of a prison cell if it gets to the right party.

The Nations trial adds up to a jolt in the state's solar plexus, a body blow to morality in government. The Kansas attorney general has called for a transcript of the Nations trial, which he plans to analyze to determine what, if any, action needs to be taken by his office. This is his duty.

If there is a lesson to be learned from the Nations trial, it is that we need to keep a closer watch on what may appear to be irregularities in all avenues of state administration, and to let no great time elapse before acting where the need for action is indicated."

* * * * *

That particular Sunday, May 26th, happened to be my mother's 48th birthday. Those supposed gods of political fortune had evidently targeted her for agony rather than celebration. My memory has stored and sealed most specifics of the events on her special day. Perhaps we had a modest cake with candles. Maybe we serenaded her with "Happy Birthday." One thing I do recall is that there were none of the usual shiny bows on carefully wrapped packages. My sisters and I had no energy to produce them. Our mother might not have possessed the will to open them even if we had.

Her birthday launched what seemed like an interminable wait for the verdicts from Attorney General Ferguson and U.S. District Attorney George concerning Annas Brown's pair of lawyers. The officials might impose extremely harsh punishment, including disbarment from the practice of law.

My recollection of that turbulent time was the sense of a suspended death sentence. It felt as if my father's identity as an attorney and politician was dangling in space like a live wire. His political superiors could either choose to electrocute him or to send out a rescue squad.

I did not know what to say to him as all of this was transpiring. He exuded little of the one-time bravado. Yet he did not appear crestfallen or depressed. No circles lolled beneath his eyes. No turndown mouth indicated trauma. He and my mother seemed to have become sudden strangers. During the scant time he was at home on weekends, they politely asked each other at dinner to pass the salt shaker, or discussed the weather. Their eyes did not meet.

Memory advises me that she was a brooding, shadowy figure. Perhaps she was spent, decimated by disgrace and devoid of energy to protest any longer.

His lack of affect, one way or the other, was puzzling. But then maybe he was preoccupied with starring as a villain in a stage play that he had authored. Even so, I could not conjure the courage to ask my burning questions: Do you feel ashamed? Are you sorry that this happened? Why did you get involved?

I did notice that he never mentioned Freddie. Dear pal. Political crony. Predecessor in the governor's chair. Surely my father must have felt an excruciating blow when the dear friend he had helped become governor testified that he knew nothing of a bribe, and claimed to have fired him as Corporation Commission counsel for his role in it. This man, who had once dined on Walnut Street and tossed the plum of an inaugural speech my father's way, acted in court as if his longtime political ally were a despicable stranger.

In our own way, during the ordeal, my sisters and I might have been strangers of sorts, too. We absolutely refused to discuss a scandal that was scalding each of us. We failed to suggest to each other that maybe

Mom had been right all along in labeling politicians as dishonest and a bunch of phonies. We did not break down and cry in front of each other about our respective aches. And we never once considered confronting our parents to vent our internal rage and pain.

Our father's repeated DO NOT admonitions, combined with Mom's molding of us as perfect political daughters, had added up to inhibition. Each member of The Harem wore the unemotional political facade that had been instilled. The composed images we paraded in front of strangers, and one another, had absolutely nothing to do with what existed behind our exteriors.

Only Hattie refused to doubt that her Paul Andrew might have erred. She chose to view the fact that his name was plastered across newspaper front pages as indication that he was more politically prominent than ever.

* * * * *

In the end, those arbitrary gods who had consistently seemed to tolerate my father's naughtiness and deviousness prevailed. Two prestigious and politically connected Kansas attorneys stepped forward and volunteered to provide supportive testimony as to his good character and legal prowess. As a result, no disciplinary action was imposed on him or Clair Hyter by either state official.

So the trauma would have seemed to be over. Jurors had long since dispersed and returned to their interrupted lives. The trial's various attorneys had refocused on new legal cases. Courtroom observers had scattered to relate gossipy trial tidbits to others. Annas Whitlow Brown remained a free woman, at least for awhile. And Starling Mack Nations could walk proudly as an honest citizen again.

Yet not everyone fared as well following the verdict. Fred Hall, whose portrait still hangs in the Kansas Supreme Court chambers, had seen his gubernatorial conduct further besmirched. Though he had returned to California, he could not have repressed the humiliation of being ridiculed in the state where he had once ruled supreme. Yet his hubris would not allow defeat. He would go on to seek the Republican nomination to the U.S. Senate and suffer yet another political defeat, this one to Californian George Murphy.

His public disgrace was minor compared to that of attorneys Hyter and Lackie.

The trial and its scandal had decimated my father's legal reputation and personal credibility. Our aspiring governor had also turned The Harem and his Snooky into pariahs at the conclusion of his crooked quest for political fame.

None of us could predict where he was headed after this fiasco. All I knew was that fantasy and ambition had become so intertwined with his reality that anything seemed plausible. As far as I could tell, only one facet of him had remained constant through all of the turmoil. It seemed certain that he would never be able to forsake completely his gubernatorial dream, regardless how his next chapter was written. He and his vision had become the same.

He would carry his illusion as one might a treasured photo of a dead person during his cross-country odyssey, which was about to commence. He would talk about it with strangers and alter facts to fit the circumstances.

I was to learn the reality of this one future day when a psychiatrist would telephone me from a distant city. My father had become his patient. And the confused physician was attempting to unravel who this person was.

The doctor would tell me that my father had been carrying on at rather great length about Kansas politics, his chairmanship of the Young Republicans, and his considerable power behind a governor. He had even spoken, quite convincingly, about being governor himself.

He would pause, awaiting my response. When I remained silent, he would ask, "Was your father ever the governor of Kansas?"

POSTSCRIPT

FAREWELL TO DASHED DREAMS
1989

"For when the One Great Scorer
Comes to write against your name
He writes - not that you won or lost
But how you played the game."

"A SOAB'S MOTTO"
Member: P.A. Lackie

Paul Andrew Lackie, Republican devotee and aspiring governor of Kansas, lived out his final days in a motel room back home in Mac. He resided there surrounded by political memorabilia as well as personal memories he chose to edit.

By then, many of the women who adored him had gone away. My mother had finally chosen freedom over further agonies and divorced him. He had lost his second wife, a Southern Baptist teetotaler, to cancer. Even Hattie, the woman he had depended on most, deserted him. She had experienced one final Spell and departed into her long anticipated "beyond" to rest forevermore in a Mac mausoleum.

One other woman, who came after all of them, shadowed him to the end. Janine was in her 40s, three decades younger than my father. She abandoned her husband and children in Oklahoma to live with him in Mac for awhile. At his funeral, she would appear to present a shocking codicil to his will. Perhaps he knew all along that she was duping him. Perhaps not.

* * * * *

204

Decades of imbibing had eaten away at his brain cells and resulted in a condition named Korsakoff's syndrome. An Oklahoma psychiatrist had phoned me one evening to announce the diagnosis. It was after my father had landed in another hospital detox ward.

I had already sensed that chunks of him seemed to be falling in different directions. He was chasing himself all over the country, seemingly adrift in the world of invisible demons where Hattie had resided for most of her life. He was running away with increasing frequency, fleeing questions he did not want to confront.

Even so, the psychiatrist's pronouncement of the Korsakoff diagnosis had caused me to slump against a wall in my apartment several hundred miles away.

He had said that my father lived in a world of grandiose delusions. It was a place populated by people who led exciting lives, had frequent dalliances with beautiful women, enjoyed enormous wealth and risky deals. "Confabulation" or invented stories, he called it. He also spoke of memory loss and impaired thinking. My father would never function properly again on his own, he had predicted.

Struggling to absorb the news, I could not help but visualize him curling those lips and scoffing as the doctor had described his condition.

* * * * *

At first, post-diagnosis, he had seemed to defy the medical odds. He had given up the "sauce" again. Then he had bought a house less than two blocks from our Walnut Street one in Mac and acquired his house mate Janine.

His predicted delusions had mainly involved politics. During weekly phone calls to me, he still referred to being "GUVVV-UH-NUH UF THIS GRAAA-TE STATE OF KANNN-SUS." He had rambled on about national politics or engaged in diatribes about the current Kansas

205

governor. Or he had reminisced about his Young GOP chairman days and speculated about the political world in general.

Neither alcohol nor defeat nor Korsakoff's syndrome had seemed able to dull the political convictions that once convinced The Harem to invest in his dream.

I had been relieved to learn that he was moving back to our home town. Maybe it meant that he would finally perch permanently in one place. I had figured he was lured back by Perry's perpetual question: "Why would anybody in their right mind want to live anywhere but Mac?" Perhaps being back home meant that he was finally forsaking the chaotic alcohol-fueled existence that had ensued after his political downfall in a Wichita courtroom.

For reasons my sisters and I could never understand, my mother had followed him cross-country after the trial. Their zigzag trail led first to Buffalo, New York, where he had found work. He had chosen a Mafia-controlled apartment building. Shapely tenants paraded hallways in fur-trimmed baby dolls while waiting for their male companions to conclude business meetings, which were conducted in red velvet chairs over cigars and Italian cuisine in a room off the lobby. Before long, my father had sought comfort in the arms of one of the prostitutes. She was a statuesque dame with mounds of platinum hair. He had nicknamed her "Mistee Flame."

Like his previous jobs, the Buffalo one had vanished suddenly with no mention of an ugly firing or cordial dismissal. He had simply announced that it was time to move on. His next position was to be in Pennsylvania. Once again, Mom had packed their bags. But the emotional momentum to salvage herself was building.

Late one night in Pennsylvania, she had received a phone call from an Episcopal rector in Ohio. He had reported that my father, near delirium, knocked at the blood-red doors of his church complaining of pain after kicking his car tires in a fit of rage. She had thanked this Good Samaritan who rescued him. Abruptly, she had faced the fact that her

27-year infatuation with that dashing Navy officer and would-be governor was over. It had made her get in her car, head back to Kansas, and
divorce my father on grounds of "gross neglect of duty."

* * * * *

Ink had barely dried on divorce papers obliterating my parents' union
when he acquired a new bride. Sara Jane was a black-eyed Southern
Baptist with a syrupy accent whom he had dubbed his "Indian Jew."
Her intent had been to reform him. "Yoh dad-eee is Gahh-d's prr-ah-
miss to meee," she had told me over long distance. "Ahhh-m goh-nnn
ta keeep him an the str-aaate an nah-row."

After parking his bride in an Oklahoma condominium, he had set
off across the Southern states in search of legal work. He had dispensed
business cards advertising his abilities: "Title Attorney. Independent
Petroleum Landman. Titles. Right-of-Way. Leasing Oil, Gas, Coal."
Each night, he had transferred that portable residence from his Cadillac
trunk to arrange it in some anonymous motel room. Such settings had
always seemed to comfort him more than any grand bedroom ever
could.

* * * * *

Death, which had been among Hattie's lifelong obsessions, finally
claimed my grandmother in January of her 84th year.

We had gathered in the Mac funeral home where she gave birth to
my father. A minister, who never met her, had volunteered that Hattie
lived "a long and useful life." He had not known about her childhood
spent with seven siblings and immigrant parents in a farm house lashed
by raging winds, scorching heat, fickle rain, giant grasshoppers, and
prairie fires. Nor had he been able to speak of her extraordinary father, who started out penniless and toiled until he could buy the funeral

house showplace in Mac and a farm for each of his children. And even if he had known, the minister probably would not have mentioned that the deceased had lived her adult life as a terrified recluse in a house bolted and barricaded against possible intruders.

Following her funeral, we had deposited Hattie in the Mac mausoleum. She had chosen it herself because no strangers could enter its locked doors or tread the ground above her. My father had participated in the ceremonies like a robot, seemingly numb to the fact that his mother's circle of protection throughout his 56 years was shattered.

Hattie's departure had forged a new bond between my father and Perry that was never possible during her totalitarian reign as a mother. My father had popped into Mac for frequent visits to drive Perry to the mausoleum or collect the cash Hattie once dispensed.

Eventually, my father and Sara Jane had moved Perry out of Mac to live near them. He had transferred his kitchen corner of rubber bands, paper clips, pipe cleaners and other miscellanea to a single room of a once-grand boarding house. Its front porch had sloped almost as erratically as the floor in our dining room back in Indy.

I had visited Perry there the year he turned 96. He would be leaving us in a matter of months to join Hattie at the mausoleum. My grandfather was tired of living, but his potent internal agonies had refused to wilt. During my visit, he had seemed fervent about speaking to me of his role in the Annas Brown affair. He still felt tremendous guilt about its having thwarted his son's gubernatorial chances. He had even trotted out a story of following his teen-age son to the Mac pool hall, and trying to discipline him like a real father. He had broached the topic of alcohol abuse, too, saying that Hattie refused to acknowledge it because she considered her Paul Andrew perfect.

Then he had offered an astonishing confession.

"Your mother phoned me after the divorce and asked, 'Why didn't you step in and do something about Hattie spoiling Paul, and letting him think he was flawless?'" Perry had added, "She said things might have turned out far differently if only I had confronted her." His eyes had welled with tears.

"I told your mother that I couldn't fight both of them," Perry had told me in a wavering voice. "Not both Hattie and Paul Andrew."

* * * * *

The family deaths had kept coming. My mother had been next, whisked away at 64 by a cancer that claimed her two months after its diagnosis. She had married a former high school suitor and settled on his Kansas farm. She had also endured another family suicide. This time, it had been her oldest brother. Grandma Ida, heartbroken and depleted by the tragedy, had given up her will to survive after that and died at 93.

During my mother's final pain-ridden days, she and I had tiptoed around our old grievances and put salve on mutual wounds. We had spoken gently of mistakes and forgiveness. She claimed to have stayed with my father for the sake of The Harem. She had said that she felt pity, rather than hatred, toward him. I could have sworn that currents of love had swirled in her voice as she delivered one last "That's enough" look.

At her funeral, a bouquet of yellow roses had appeared with a card signed: "Cynthia, Margo, and Andrea." It had made me think of the arm load of buttercup yellow long stems my father presented his Snooky to christen her dream house on Walnut Street. Afterward, I had asked whether he sent the roses. He had answered by lighting a cigarette with a trembling hand as his eyes gyrated about the room.

* * * * *

Then Sara Jane had deserted my father via death with little warning. He had decided to bury his Southern belle in Mac despite the fact she despised the "downnn-raht chi-llly" winters of Kansas. At the funeral home, he had presided as if hosting a cocktail party. He had rushed about her open casket to rearrange flowers while muttering about her overdone makeup and black bouffant "do." I had watched and wondered what would become of him now that his Southern Baptist anchor had vanished.

No sooner had the funeral ended than my question was answered. Abandoned with neither a wife nor mother to prop him up, he had turned to me. It was as if all of our years together had suddenly evaporated and I was the little girl expected to cooperate with whatever he wanted. As usual, he had tried to seduce me with words and coerce me to his side.

At Sara Jane's grave site, he had begged me to drive him in the Cadillac from Mac to Oklahoma. His eyesight was deteriorating, he had said. His tone had implied a potential auto accident. "Please, Mrs. Tusswagon." He had offered a woeful look. Like a fish being reeled in to have its head and tail cut off, I had succumbed.

Shortly after our marathon trip had begun, it turned into a blur. There were hourly truck stop intermissions for coffee and pie. Cigarette ashes overflowed the Cadillac tray as country western lyrics reverberated on the radio. Political platitudes spilled forth on an array of issues. My head had started to pound on a journey that seemed to have no destination with a companion who was unable to stop talking.

Perhaps our trip had been fortuitous though. This had been the first concentrated dose of time I spent alone with him since high school. It had only verified the sentiments that I began facing back then. All traces of my one-time ability to endorse his grandiose political fantasies and personal promises had disappeared. Somewhere back along our torturous path together, he had lost me as his lead cheerleader. My response to him had become obligatory and restrained. I had realized that I could drive him from one state to another and even feel sorry for him. But I could no longer mesh my soul with his.

Margo, as usual, had been a step ahead of me. Some time before, she had established sufficient emotional distance from my father that he

210

would never consider trying to access her as readily as me. His political scandal had irreversibly wounded her.

My bright and lovely sister had encountered his political notoriety more than a year after the trial's end during rush week for University of Kansas sororities. Their "Remember who you are and what you represent" mottos had forbidden inclusion of a girl tainted by scandal. Though I had tried to reassure Margo that this rejection of her was arbitrary and random, not personal, we both suspected that was not true.

Later, she would say of that painful time during which she had come to dislike our father intensely: "I felt so protective toward Mom. It (the scandal) was everything she dreaded, all about what people thought of you. It absolutely ruined all of our lives."

Andrea had observed Margo's agony and selected a Kansas college far away from Lawrence when her turn came. She had hoped that people there might have forgotten about the scandal. A sorority had accepted her. But she had soon left school and, like the rest of us, continued to grapple with the aftermath of shame inflicted on our family.

* * * * *

In July of my father's 73rd year, I received the phone call concerning his death. It came at Mac's Red Coach Inn motel, where he had resided since selling the house he shared with Janine. Like every other motel, he had adored this one. The Coacher, he had called it. "Finest establishment in Mac," he had liked to say. "So glad I haven't alienated anyone here. Mac is a great place to come home to."

He had departed the world sober and in bed wearing designer jeans, boxer shorts, and white socks. To this day, I cannot fathom my sartorially impeccable dad sleeping in his clothes. The official cause of death was arteriosclerosis. It was recorded by a Mac coroner who did not arrive at The Coacher until eight hours later.

211

His single motel room had a flimsy door opening to an indoor cement courtyard that surrounded a swimming pool. He had dubbed this attraction his "living room" and spent hours there haranguing confounded guests about his political theories. He had raved about its restaurant, too. The chirpy waitresses, plastic posies on laminated tabletops, and coffee seemingly devoid of caffeine had delighted him. He had even boasted about the prominent sign advertising homemade pie and rolls.

In his cramped room, he had created a miniature version of Hattie's jammed spaces. Chairs, tables, and a bed vied for space atop the blue carpet. His closet overflowed with suits in dry cleaner plastic. The bathroom was heaped with toiletries. The scent of his sweet cologne and stale tobacco infiltrated everything. Piles of papers sat everywhere. Tabletops featured pictures of him and Hattie. I expected him to appear at any minute to pronounce as he used to about the Marlin Street living room: "Just like living in a furniture store." I also had the eerie sensation that my grandmother might be hovering there as a ghostly presence.

His funeral took place on a sweltering July day. My sisters and I sat on folding chairs with our backs facing a smattering of mourners. As the minister droned, jagged sobs erupted somewhere behind us. They competed with his voice and caused me to swivel in my seat. My eyes traveled across lines of mostly empty chairs to a woman sitting on the back row. A black veil covered her face. My stares prompted her to jump up and flee onto the heat-parched streets of Mac.

At the cemetery, the woman in black reappeared. She leaned into a tree near his grave site. Hot fingers of wind whipped at her veil but failed to uncover her face. She issued more noisy sobs that caused everyone in the small group of bystanders to glance her way.

Though my father certainly would have preferred to depart life as a former governor of Kansas, I knew that the theatrics of his funeral would have pleased him. He would have relished the drama of his final

212

appearance featuring a mystery mourner, the startled folks from Mac, his bewildered relatives, and his loyal VFW cronies in patriotic uniforms. I could envision him buzzing about to greet each of these characters. Smoke would be trailing his silk suit. He would be as giddy as if starring at one of his political rallies.

I knew that I should be weeping as his casket descended slowly into the earth. Instead, I thought of how much he would hate being banished outdoors to spend forever all alone with no audience to consider his remarks. Instead of tears spilling from my eyes, I felt beads of sweat trickling down my nylons.

The funereal drama followed my sisters and me to the Coacher after the burial. Janine, who proved to be the veiled mystery weeper, phoned to say that she was staying two doors away from my father's room. She advised, in a voice husky from cigarettes, that she needed to present a codicil to his will.

We met by the courtyard pool. She handed me a list penciled on notebook paper. It awarded her his Cadillac, plus an odd assortment of small items. She wanted the car immediately, Janine said. Inky eyes flashed at me above a clenched jaw. She seemed to personify my father's description of a "hard-lookin' woman." And there was one more thing she would like me to hand over to her.

"I want your father's undershirts," she said.

I stared at her. My thoughts careened. She claimed to have written the codicil herself while he dictated it. His hands shook too much for him to do it himself, she said. But he had signed it, she insisted. Examining the wavering signature, I supposed it could have been his. It was true that his writing had been nearly indecipherable for years. Surely she could not have had the nerve to forge it.

"You will have to wait awhile for the car," I told her, struggling for an authoritative tone. "I need to talk with our attorney first."

Back in his Coacher room, my sisters and I joked about our father's female entourage. Yet beneath my "Leave it to Dad" and "Can you believe it?" cracks flowed a resentment about having to deal with his excesses once again. He might as well have been alive in that motel room with us and chuckling at my consternation about having to clean up another of his messes.

In a weak moment some time before, I had agreed to be his estate executor. He had insisted that all the arrangements were in place. The task would be clear-cut and simple. Yet the estate quagmire he had left me to resolve was missing several puzzle pieces and would get even murkier. While sorting his effects, I discovered that an heirloom family diamond and parts of his coin collection were missing. The motel manager said my father had feared that Janine possessed the copy of a key to his room. I was also to learn that he neglected to mention a joint $25,000 insurance policy she and my father had purchased on his life.

So it fell to me to present all of these embarrassing tidbits to the estate attorney.

"UNDERSHIRTS?" His eyes dilated behind his glasses. "She wants your father's undershirts?" After recovering, he suggested that handwriting experts should assess the authenticity of the codicil signature. Skeptically, I agreed. Time would reveal that he had been right. Two handwriting analysts concluded that Janine did forge the codicil.

Later on, it would be discovered that she had also defaulted on one of the monthly life insurance payments. Negligence had cost her $25,000. The mystery of the missing diamond ring and coins was never to be resolved.

The task I dreaded most in disposing of my father's belongings involved his voluminous papers. By the time I got to them, I loathed The Coacher. It sickened me that this had been his final setting. It was not so much the motel's stench of pool chlorine wafting throughout or the general tackiness of everything. It had to do with the vision of my father, who had once paraded about in silk suits and mesmerized crowds, living there behind a cheap motel room door and finding pleasure in the dreary Coacher coffee shop.

214

All of it conjured Margo's one-time comparison of our father with the golden-tongued, scandalous Elmer Gantry. "Dad always identified with hurdy-gurdy, flimflam types," she said.

My father's final paper trail related only part of his life story. He had saved one copy of every single newspaper that chronicled his political aspirations and glories. His countenance stared back at me from yellowed newsprint with mastheads from all over his beloved Kansas. Atop the newspaper heap was a December 8, 1949, McPherson newspaper with the headline "Lackie Young GOP Head" accompanied by gushing praise:

> "...The McPherson County News congratulates
> Paul on his victory ... McPherson should be proud of
> the fact that a local boy has attained a position of such
> worth and importance in a state organization."

With the newspapers were letters from governors and other political notables, newspaper editorials with his scribbling in the margins, photos from various Republican events, and even that Abe medal from the Chicago convention. All of his gubernatorial potential had come to rest there in those faded and musty paper piles.

Conspicuously absent among his treasured newspaper clips was all mention of his one-time pal, Freddie. More than two decades before, in 1966, Fred Hall had suffered a stroke. Four years later, at age 54, the politician once described as a "young man in too big a hurry" had died. That rush to grab the prize was one more trait the former friends had shared.

Inside a jammed dresser drawer he had stashed a selective segment of his amorous pursuits. Gushing wartime letters to my mother and me kept company with naughty Navy-era calling cards. They advertised: "Paul A. Lackie, I'd Leave My Happy Home 4-U" or "Office Hours From 1 Till Won." It sickened me to consider the image of my mother sitting alone at home in Mac while he had engaged in romantic overseas conquests.

There were tattered letters and greeting cards from a college girl named Mavis. Love tomes from Sara Jane described him as "my world to eternity." There was also a recent letter from someone named Velma who referred to an expected engagement ring from him.

Buried in that stack of correspondence lay a letter addressed to "Dear Mrs. Tusswagon." It had been written on thin tissue paper for my fifth birthday. From his Navy ship, my father had penned me his reflections about war and patriotism:

> " ... And it is only thru hope that my being away now will make your lives, and those of other children and parents everywhere, happier in days to come ... Some day you will probably know that your Daddy, and the fellows with him ... were away working for a dream that maybe hasn't come true - But you must always continue to dream, and to believe in your dreams, because believing in dreams is what makes so many of them come true."

A stranger who might have thumbed through his papers could never have known about the chunks of his life he had chosen to delete. The political payoff scandal might never have occurred. He had banished it from his effects just as Hattie did threatening strangers from her house.

No traces remained, either, of all the women who had subscribed to his vows that he would strike it rich and win the election and beat the bottle and become governor. No evidence existed that Josie, with her pink apartment and Swedish angel face, had been his love goddess. Janine, with her undershirt and Cadillac yearnings, had been deleted as well.

All memories of my mother, other than some of his letters to her, had vanished, too. He had not saved a single photo of her or anything referring to their 27 years as husband and wife. In the deep reaches of my memory, I could still glimpse my mother's rapturous face and shining eyes back when she had idolized my father. I remembered Sara Jane wearing a similar glow in his presence. Josie, too, must have felt their same rush of excitement at the prospect of residing in his universe of infinite possibilities. Janine had even deserted her family for him.

What none of these women who had longed to possess him could have suspected was that such ownership was impossible. Each of them had arrived too late. Another woman had already staked her exclusive claim long before these aspirants came along. She had named him Paul Andrew, walked him to grade school daily beneath a protective umbrella, baked him cherry pies, bankrolled his political dreams, and pronounced him perfect. As he often said of her: "She spoiled me rotten."

The only female ever to possess him had summarized her eternal devotion in a birthday note penciled on an index card. He had carried it with him always. It had sat propped on his motel bedside table the night he died. Hattie had written:

> "To My Dearest Treasure
> in all the big World.
> With Heaps of good Wishes
> For many Happy Birthdays.
> From Your mother
> To Paul Andrew Lackie
> May 8 - 1937."

Cynthia Dennis is an award-winning journalist, and graduate of the University of Kansas. She spent nearly two decades as a feature writer and columnist for Wisconsin's largest newspaper, taught journalism while obtaining a master's degree in mass communications at the University of Wisconsin-Milwaukee, and has written for magazines, radio and television.